REASONABLE DOUBTS

IS YOUR FAITH BUILT ON FACT OR FICTION?

BY R. SCOTT RICHARDS

THE WORD FOR TODAY

P.O. Box 8000, Costa Mesa, CA 92628

Reasonable Doubts
Is Your Faith Built on Fact or Fiction?
by R. Scott Richards
Published by **The Word for Today**
P.O. Box 8000, Costa Mesa, CA 92628

ISBN 0–936728–60–4

© 1996 The Word for Today

TABLE OF CONTENTS

ACKNOWLEDGMENTS

Special thanks go out to a number of people who were instrumental in seeing this project come to pass.

To my wife Pam, who is a constant living illustration of the love of God.

To my family for teaching me to love to read, to think, and to laugh.

To Dick Richards who went above and beyond the call of duty as commentator, advisor, and father.

To Chuck Smith, who taught me the meaning of grace.

Without these invaluable contributions, this book would exist only in the realm of "might–have–been."

PREFACE

In II Timothy 4:3–4 the Bible tells us that "the time will come when men will not endure sound doctrine, but wanting to have their ears tickled, they will accumulate for themselves teachers in accordance with their own desires, and will turn away their ears from the truth and turn aside to myths."

There are few predictions in the Word of God that are being more directly fulfilled in our day than this one. Many people are basing their hope of eternal life on a dangerously distorted concept of truth that bears only the slightest resemblance to the actual teaching of Scripture.

Reasonable Doubts is an insightful and entertaining look at a series of false teachings that are often taken for the Gospel truth in our culture. As you read *Reasonable Doubts*, you may find a number of the ideas you take most for granted about God shaken to their foundations. You may find some effective ways to reach those who have been led astray. But you will never be able to look at the spiritual confusion that rules our day in quite the same way again.

Chuck Smith
Calvary Chapel of Costa Mesa

CHAPTER I
MYTHS THE WORLD TAUGHT ME

The biggest liar in the world is "They Say."
— Douglas Malloch —

STOP ME if you've heard this one before...

Hot Dog!
It seems there was this old lady who had been given a microwave oven by her children. After bathing her dog she put it in the microwave to dry it off. Naturally, when she opened the door the dog was cooked from the inside out. [1]

The Kentucky Fried Rat
Two couples stopped one night at a notable carryout for a fried chicken snack. The husband returned to the car with the chicken. While sitting there in the car eating their chicken, his wife said, "My chicken tastes funny." She continued to eat and continued to complain. After a while the husband said, "Let me see it." He cut the light on and discovered that the woman was eating a rodent, nicely floured and fried crisp. The woman went into shock and was rushed to the hospital. [2]

The Philanderer's Porsche
A man in California saw an ad in the paper for an "almost new" Porsche, in excellent condition—price

$50. He was almost certain the printers had made a typographical error, but even at $5,000 it would have been a bargain, so he hummed to the address to look at the car. A nice–looking woman appeared at the front door. Yes, she had placed the ad. The price was indeed $50. "The car," she said, "is in the garage. Come and look at it." The fellow was overwhelmed. It was a beautiful new Porsche, and, as the ad promised, "nearly new." He asked if he could drive the car around the block. The woman said, "Of course," and went with him. The Porsche drove like a dream. The young man peeled off $50 and handed it over, somewhat sheepishly. The woman gave him the necessary papers, and the car was his. Finally, the new owner couldn't stand it any longer. He had to know why the woman was selling the Porsche at such a ridiculously low price. Her reply was simple: With a half smile on her face, she said, "My husband ran off with his secretary a few days ago and left a note instructing me to sell the car and the house, and send him the money."[3]

These harrowing accounts are familiar turf for most of us. At one time or another we've heard them recounted with minor twists and variations and embellishments. We may have vaguely recalled reading about these events in the newspaper, or hearing about them through television or radio, or perhaps they were dramatically shared in hushed tones around the water cooler at work. But the remarkable accounts of "Hot Dog," "The Kentucky Fried Rat," and "The Philanderer's Porsche" all have one thing in common: None of them is true.

Jan Harold Brunvand, an English professor at the University of Utah includes these and many other familiar "true life adventures" in his insightful book, *The Vanishing Hitchhiker: American Urban Legends and Their Meanings.*

Legends? Modern myths and fanciful tales growing and flourishing in our sophisticated, media–saturated, highly educated society? Didn't that sort of thing go out with Viking raiding parties and Fred Flintstone–like individuals huddling around a tiny campfire at night?

Don't bet on it. After years of study, Dr. Brunvand came to this conclusion:

> *It might seem unlikely that legends, urban legends at that—would continue to be created in an age of widespread literacy, rapid mass communications, and restless travel. While our pioneer ancestors may have had to rely heavily on oral tradition to pass the news along about changing events and frontier dangers, surely we no longer need mere "folk" reports of what's happening with all their tendencies to distort the facts. A moment's reflection, however, reminds us of the many weird, fascinating, but unverified rumors and tales that so frequently come to our ears— killers and madmen on the loose, shocking or funny personal experiences, unsafe manufactured products, and many other unexplained mysteries of daily life. Sometimes we encounter different oral versions of such stories, and on occasion we may read about similar events in newspapers or magazines; but seldom do we find, or even seek after, reliable documentation. The lack of verification in no way diminishes the appeal urban legends have for us.... And the legends we tell, as with any folklore, reflect many of the hopes, fears, and anxieties of our time. In short, legends are definitely part of our modern folklore—legends which are as traditional, variable, and functional as those of the past.[4]*

You Ain't Seen Nuthin' Yet

Clearly, myths, legends, and half–truths are a cherished part of contemporary life. But consider for a moment an unsettling possibility. Such modern folklore may be having a greater influence on our thinking than any of us would care to admit. While we're on the subject of tall tales, let me offer a few more vague, unverifiable, yet ardently believed legends of our own times:

- "God helps those who help themselves."
- "Man is basically good."
- "The Bible is full of errors."
- "The true meaning of Christmas is togetherness."
- "It doesn't matter what you believe as long as you're sincere."
- "Jesus was a blond–haired, blue–eyed mystic."

If you believe that any of the above statements are "the gospel truth" you may be in for a shock. The objective evidence, contained not only in the pages of the Bible but also in the realm of day–to–day experience, argues strongly against the notions contained in these spiritual sounding *bon mots.* Yet ironically, many that I have had the opportunity to converse with about a relationship with God consider these sorts of sentiments the rough equivalent of the "fundamentals of the faith." Could it possibly be that our day will be remembered as a time of unprecedented spiritual interest and unprecedented spiritual ignorance as well?

Taking Our Spiritual Pulse

They call it McPaper.

Let's face it, for a daily newspaper to be likened to a fast food restaurant may not be the highest form of praise. But, like that friendly purveyor of Big Macs and super–size fries, *USA Today* is doing quite well, thank you. With a daily circulation of nearly one and a half million readers, this collection of short news reports and high–tech color graphics must be touching a nerve.

Perhaps the secret of *USA Today's* success is its ability to involve the average reader as part of the news of the day. Our culture places great stock in being trendy. Knowing what the average man on the street thinks about current issues is very important to us. *USA Today* responds to this felt need by providing an endless parade of overnight polls. At times these surveys merely state the obvious, but on occasion the results are genuinely startling.

One such eye–opening study was done prior to the visit of Pope John Paul II to North America in 1987. In an article titled "We Search for Spiritual Well–Being," 61 percent of adults stated that religion was very important in their lives. Fifty–five percent read the Bible at least once a month, 63 percent prayed on a regular basis, and 81 percent of those with children believed it was very to extremely important to rear them with religion. A whopping 74 percent stated that they felt spiritually fulfilled. Religious interest was definitely on the upswing as 35 percent indicated that spiritual concerns meant more to them than five years earlier. Results such as these could lead us to the conclusion that our generation is both deeply committed to God and knowledgeable about spiritual matters.

Why should anyone find such a keenly felt sense of spiritual concern in America startling? After all, we put "In God We Trust" on our money. We celebrate the holidays like Thanksgiving and Christmas. We are guaranteed the freedom to worship as our conscience dictates. Why should a healthy response to a religious interest survey be thought of as unexpected?

Let's compare our *USA Today* findings with another poll. According to the Gallup organization, nine out of ten Americans said they have never doubted the existence of God. Eight out of ten agreed that "we will all be called before God at the Judgment Day to answer for our sins." Eighty–one percent considered themselves Christians. So far, so good. But when the Gallup people began to get specific about faith, the responses took an unexpected turn. Only 42 percent of those surveyed knew that Jesus delivered the Sermon on the Mount. Less than half were able to name the authors of the four Gospels. A mere 37 percent believed that the Bible is infallible, and when asked what book has had the greatest influence on their

lives, barely more than 1 percent mentioned the Bible.
George Gallup Jr. comments:

> *Now, these disparate survey items are not only
> interesting in themselves—and perhaps, in
> some cases, shocking—but they also shed
> light, I believe, on the complex picture of
> religion in America today:*
>
> * *the widespread appeal or popularity of
>   religion;*
> * *the glaring lack of knowledge;*
> * *the inconsistencies of belief;*
> * *in part, the failure of organized religion in
>   some respects to make a difference in our
>   society.*[5]

What are we to think about such starkly contrasting
results? It seems evident that as a culture, we major on
spiritual sentiment and virtually dismiss the importance of
spiritual content. Our motto seems to be: if it feels good–
believe in it!

When the Chickens Come Home to Roost

In my experience working with university students, I
have seen this tendency affect both Christians and non–
Christians in a dramatic way. One evening I was taking
part in an open discussion of the claims of Christ at the
University of Arizona. The group interaction had be lively
and positive. As the meeting progressed, I noticed that one
young woman had come in late and was keeping a
comfortable distance toward the back of the crowd. The
meeting time was drawing to a close, and I began to share
a brief biblical overview of what it meant to know God in a
personal way. As I was in mid–sentence, the relaxed
atmosphere of the group was shattered. In an angry and
confident voice, the late–arriving visitor shouted, "Hey! I
believe that Jesus was a liar!" The focus of attention in the
room jolted to this young woman and then rebounded
straight back to me. To call this unexpected outburst a
minor distraction would be like calling the Super Bowl a

minor media event. The question surging through everyone's mind in the group (including my own) was "How do you deal with a tense, confrontive situation like this?"

Pausing for a moment to clear my throat, I responded, "That's a very strong statement. What has led you to that conclusion?"

She seemed confused by my question, but shot back, "I think Jesus was a liar, and you can't prove that he's not!"

I replied, "I understand your position. I just want to know why you believe it. What is it about Jesus' life or His teaching that makes you believe that He is a liar?"

"You mean something specific?"

"Yes. Have you ever read the eyewitness accounts of Christ's life in the New Testament?"

"Well... no."

Meanwhile, Back in the Pews

Too often our lack of basic spiritual understanding prevents us from seriously and rationally coming to grips with the person of Jesus Christ. Sadly, this same tendency can work like a time bomb in the life of even a committed Christian. Living in a city with a major university presents both challenges and opportunities for those who work with students. One of the major challenges is so predictable we've even given it a semi–scientific name: "Distraught–church–kid–meets–the–big–bad–world Syndrome" (or D.C.K.M.B.B.W.S. for short).

After years of a conflict–free, well–insulated life, filled with like–thinking Christian friends, youth groups, and schools, our candidate for D.C.K.M.B.B.W.S. boldly goes to the campus of a secular university. Like many others, he will spend his first day in class watching in shocked silence as a profanity–spewing humanities professor slices, dices, and makes coleslaw of his often untested and seldom–thought–through beliefs.

For the first time in his life, our fledgling believer is caught adrift in a brave new post–Christian world. He finds himself being intensely questioned about his seemingly antiquated worldview and sadly at a loss for answers. He soon learns that well–worn Christian cliches won't cut it. He begins to go into a kind of spiritual vapor lock. He simply doesn't know how to respond. This rude awakening to the "real world" will have a profound impact on the spiritual well–being of our wide–eyed, innocent seeker of truth. The excitement and relevancy of his faith will soon become a dim adolescent memory. Ten years down the line he will find himself in one of two easily identifiable groups. He will become a card carrying member of either the "I'm–religious–but–I'd–rather–not–talk–about–such–a–personal–subject" club or the dreaded "Oh–yeah–I–used–to–believe–that–stuff–could–you–pass–me–another–beer" society.

Clearly, we live in a time of oddly conflicting religious attitudes. For the most part, we seem interested in knowing God, but not interested enough to discover what we believe about Him or why we believe it. The apostle Paul's words in Romans 10:2 seem like a vivid description of our spiritual environment: "For I bear them witness that they have a zeal for God, but not in accordance with knowledge."

The Next Best Thing to Knowing God

Unfortunately, where facts are lacking, fantasy floods in. Instead of investing the effort to gain a solid, fact–based perspective on crucial spiritual issues, many people buy into a fuzzy cultural consensus called American folk religion. Built on the words of modern–day prophets such as William Shakespeare ("To thine own self be true") and Benjamin Franklin ("God helps those who help themselves"), this cultural gospel is well entrenched in popular religious thought. These modern myths make up a largely unchallenged treasure trove of current conventional "wisdom" about God and ourselves.

Perhaps it's time to look at these unchallenged assumptions with a healthy dose of skepticism. Can we believe the Bible–or is it just a nice bedtime story? Is God real, or just a way of coping with the stress of life? Is there any sure way to know God, or to be sure He knows us? It has been said that truth is only found by those who refuse to settle for less. Many people are surprised to learn that the Bible commends those with such an uncompromising attitude. Speaking of a group of 1st Century truth seekers in a place called Berea, Acts 17:11 states; "these were more nobel minded than those at Thessalonica, in that they received the word with all readiness, and searched the Scriptures daily to find out whether these things were so."

Would your own set of beliefs, about God, about life, about the afterlife stand up under that kind of examination? Are you certain, beyond a reasonable doubt, that your faith is built on facts and not fairy tales?

In the following pages, we will attempt to expose the highly valued, popularly accepted spiritual "truths" of our day to the light of the message of the Bible. In our quest for solid answers, we will take a new look at humanity. How do we stand in relationship to God? Is He pleased with us? Will sincerity and giving our all lead us to Him after all?

We will see what the Bible says about the nature of God Himself. Are all religious roads leading in His direction? Can we simply accept Jesus as one of the many equally valid religious teachers? Can a rational person believe that Jesus was literally raised from the dead?

Finally, we will take a new look at life. Are the prizes we chase in our culture worth pursuing? Can we discover the reason God has placed us here? Is there more to a relationship with God than being a nice person and going to church?

Woody Allen is undoubtedly better known for comedy than deep philosophy. But Allen wasn't laughing when he observed, "There will be no major solution to the suffering of mankind until we reach some understanding of who we are, what the purpose of creation was, what happens after death. Until these questions are resolved we are caught." In his films, Allen makes it clear that he is doubtful that answers to our human dilemma exist.

The Bible presents a completely different point of view. Faith need not be a hopeless leap into the dark. True biblical faith is a step into the light. In the light of God's truth we can discover who we are, why we are here, and where we are going. We can encounter the fullness of life the Father has wanted for us all along.

To fulfill our deep longings for a relationship with God, we must understand the facts of spiritual life. We must not settle for the false and superficial answers so popular today. As we turn the light of truth on the realm of myth and hearsay, be prepared! We will discover real answers that very well may change the way you see God, yourself and quite possibly the meaning of life.

Discussion Questions

1. Read I Kings 18:20–39. Would you say people today are more or less spiritually committed than the people we see in this account? Explain your answer.

2. In verse 31 we discover that the altar of the Lord had been broken down. What insights can this give us into the condition of the hearts of the people? Were they hostile or indifferent to God's truth? Which attitude is tougher to deal with?

3. Have you ever encountered a person who had zeal for God, but not according to knowledge? Do such people seem happy to you? Why or why not?

4. Douglas Malloch was quoted as saying, "The biggest liar in the world is 'They say.'" Can you think of some popular ideas that you've found to be false? What kind of problems can misplaced faith lead us into?

CHAPTER II
FAITH OR FAIRY TALES?

God, why didn't you make the evidence of your existence more sufficient?
— Bertrand Russell —

"Boy, I'm glad that's him and not me."

EVER FOUND that thought running through your mind?

Maybe it was in a sixth grade math class when the teacher stared right into our rabbit–in–the headlights terrorized eyes and yet called on the poor sap sitting next to us. Maybe it was that morning we watched in shock as a colleague made the biggest proposal of his professional life with a zipper at half mast. Perhaps it was the time we noticed a blob of secret sauce that had been hitch hiking on a friend's chin since lunch three hours ago. But for me, the time I was most grateful to be standing on the sidelines during a crucial social blunder happened in the warm and wholesome surroundings of a church service on Christmas eve.

The pastor of this largish southwestern congregation had developed quite a reputation for his information dense, academically oriented sermons. This "Just the facts, ma'am" approach to speaking had led him to rely heavily on his speaking notes, with only an occasional launch out into the deep waters of an off the cuff remark. But this evening would be different. The service was billed as a get together for the entire family (three years old and up). Because of this unique audience, the sermon would take on a decidedly different informal, conversational style.

For the first fifteen minutes everyone present would have agreed that this was one great talk. Warm, open, full of easy to relate to holiday memories of family and friends. What could have been better?

But then, disaster struck.

In the middle of describing a Christmas memory from his childhood, the pastor paused. In one of those innocent, unplanned remarks that speakers usually live to regret, he looked at his audience, cleared his throat and said, "And, of course, we all know there is no such thing as Santa Claus."

As I sat in the front row, I turned and watched as a stunned reaction rolled across the auditorium. Little three to five year old eyes turned toward their parents with a look of shock and betrayal. Adult faces turned pale and then red with the same kind of anger usually reserved for flag burners or pyramid marketing scheme salesmen. At this point, the pastor might as well have been speaking to a group of Rush Limbaugh disciples on "International Communism: Let's Give It One More Try!"

One small observation, a minor, off the cuff remark had transformed Christmas Eve from a happy holiday to a credibility crisis for all ages.

As I watched a parade of disgruntled parents and disillusioned kiddies trudge out of the service I came to an important conclusion about the wacky world of the modern church. You can preach against sin, you can preach about hell, you can preach about Jesus being the only way to heaven, but whatever you do, *don't* take on Santa Claus.

Sorry, Virginia...

How did you finally come to the sad conclusion that there was no such thing as Santa Claus? Perhaps it was that Christmas when you discovered that the handwriting of the jolly old elf was suspiciously similar to Mom's. Or perhaps you uncovered a present or two from the North Pole under the tree two weeks before the big day. Maybe you took the scientific approach and tried to figure out how the fat guy managed to shimmy down your tiny excuse for a chimney. Or perhaps a little detective work revealed that along with the traditional peanut butter sandwich and cookies, Santa had the same taste in beverages as Dad.

Usually by the time our parents got up the nerve to tell us the truth we had long since figured it all out anyway. "Get real. I knew this was a scam when I was five!" (Of course we went along with the deal on the hope it meant more presents!)

Coming to the conclusion that there is no Santa Claus tends to stand out in our memories as one of those bench mark steps toward adulthood. Sure it would be nice if there really was a miniature sleigh and eight tiny reindeer, but sooner or later we have to face facts. We have to grow up and learn to live in the slightly less pleasant, slightly less wonderful world of reality.

The Great Santa In the Sky?

Interestingly, some people go through a similar process concerning their faith in God. A semester or two at a local college or university is usually enough to do the job. When we were young it made sense to believe that there was a creative genius behind the miracle we call the universe. But, after all, science and the latest issue of National Geographic assure us that all we see can be explained by natural process. Sure, it was comforting to believe that God had a plan for our lives, but now everything from MTV to Madison Avenue tells us that we can make life full and meaningful all on our own. We may have even been committed to "doing the right thing" for years, convinced that God was watching our every move. But as we strayed farther and farther from the straight and narrow, we discovered that we could sin and no divine lightning bolts would zap us on the spot. Many of us began to question whether this God who seemed so real to us as children really existed at all. Add to this a few boring Sundays in church, complete with a few less than pleasant encounters with grief or guilt dealing religious types and the conclusion became clear. God certainly was a nice concept, but not something to be taken seriously in the realm of mature, adult day–to–day life.

Too Cool for God?

Some who go through this process take things a step further and start to buy into a kind of cool cynicism toward spiritual issues. They get their kicks by turning up their nose at the whole idea of God. Some even enjoy giving the cold shoulder to those so weak and immature as to consider faith an important part of life. As writer Sean O'Casey expressed it, "I think we ought to have as great a regard for religion as we can, so as to keep it out of as many things as possible."

So what about it? Is God just a more sophisticated version of "Santy," made socially acceptable for grown ups? Or does God exist in reality independent of whether we choose to believe in Him or not? Is it possible that the One the Bible calls "I Am" is just as real as the summer sun in Tucson, rainfall in Seattle, or rush hour traffic on the D.C. Beltway?

Clearly, the existence of God is a question that deserves some serious thought. Far from a side issue or a superficial concern, our answer to this question will have far reaching impact upon our lives. If God has no more substance than a North Pole toy factory then the most practical approach to life is let's eat, drink and be merry for tomorrow we die.

The best thing that we can do is to live to stimulate our nerve endings.

But if God does exist, then there just may be an answer to the aching emptiness, the hunger for purpose and real love, the need to see beyond the icy grave that we carry with us every day of our lives.

In wrestling with the question of the existence of God, there are three major issues we must deal with personally before we can arrive at any substantial answer.

The Meaning of Proof

Have you ever noticed that certain subjects seem to have a powerful emotional charge built into them? Around a dinner table we can discuss football, fashion trends or fly fishing and have a good deal of confidence that no one will blow their stack. But if the subject of God happens to come up, nervousness takes over the room with all the subtlety of Stormin' Norman Schwartzkopf moving into Iraq.

There is a reason for all this high anxiety. The discussion of spiritual issues not only can, but does get some people hot and bothered, especially if there is a night and day difference in opinion present. Think about it. When was the last time you heard someone passively say, "You know, I'm just not sure that God exists, and I'm sincerely curious as to what has led you to conclude that He is real." More often than not our home version of Point/Counterpoint begins with an invitingly polite opener like, "Oh, Yeah?? Prove to me that God exists! I dare you!!!"

Many of us know what it feels like to be on the receiving end of that kind of statement. The stomach begins to get tight, our pulse starts to beat like Ricky Ricardo's percussion section and our instinctive reaction is to reply with a winsome, bridge building response like, "Well, if you weren't such an unchurched, sewer brained heathen destined for the ultimate weenie roast you'd know that God was real!!"

But behind all the anger and verbal mayhem of these encounters there is a legitimate question that is often ignored in the heat of battle. What would it take to prove to the average person that God exists?

More often than not, when a person asks for proof of spiritual reality, they are asking for something scientific in nature. They want something observable, testable and repeatable. Many skeptics claim they would believe if they could see God in a telescope or reduce Him to a specimen that could be measured and weighed.

Spanning the Universe

There is only one minor flaw with this seeing–is–believing school of spiritual investigation. God hasn't been in the habit of making personal appearances for lab tests. In fact, in an incredibly understated manner, the prophet Isaiah tells us that God is far beyond our limited ability to comprehend.

> Who has measured the waters in the hollow of His hand,
> And marked off the heavens by the span,
> And calculated the dust of the earth by the measure,
> And weighed the mountains in a balance,
> And the hills in a pair of scales? (Isaiah 40:12)

As we look at God from this human set of references, we begin to come to some mind boggling conclusions. This bit of divine accommodation to our view of life is staggering in its implications. Have you ever found yourself in awe of nature, even overwhelmed by its almost incomprehensible power? The Bible tells us that even the most spectacular aspects of creation pale in comparison to their Creator.

Something's Fishy Here

Isaiah begins by telling us that God is able to take all the collected water in the universe and hold it in His hand. This is a remarkable statement, especially when we stop to realize that water can be an amazingly powerful force, particularly when we find ourselves buried under large quantities of the stuff.

One day I was invited by a friend to go snorkeling in the kelp beds off a rocky beach area near Malibu, California. With our jet fins kicking away it was an easy matter to get through the surf line and make our way to the beautiful, blue green world of the kelp forest. My diving buddy, Bob, was an avid pole spear fisherman and soon had three dying bass flopping listlessly on a stringer trailing away behind him.

As a classic example of the great American sportsman, Bob couldn't have been more happy with his catch. But I was having a distinctly different reaction to his good luck. Having just watched the movie "Jaws" about two days before our trip, it wasn't hard for me to imagine that these skewered fish were sending out a dinner call to every shark within two miles of us. Finally, I mustered up enough courage to ask the classic dumb rookie diver's question.

"Uh, hey, Bob. Don't you ever worry about some jumbo sea critter coming by to help himself to your bass (and us too while we're at it)?"

Through his partially fogged diving mask I could still make out a look of exasperation, usually seen on the face of Driver's Ed teachers when a student asks, "Now, how do I get this thing into reverse?"

He sighed, spit his snorkel out of his mouth, and replied, "Listen, Scott. As soon as you set foot in the water you become part of the food chain. Besides, if something that big wants to get you, there's absolutely nothing you can do about it."

"Except maybe stay on the beach." Since this was hardly a line Lloyd Bridges would deliver on *Sea Hunt*, I decided to keep common sense to myself and continue diving.

To be honest, it was a beautiful day in the kelp forest. The visibility was a good twenty feet, with ethereal shafts of silver light streaking down through the seaweed canopy above. There was a good population of dark blue, green and even bright orange fish to chase. Soon I found myself becoming more and more adventurous, diving closer and closer to the rock strewn floor some 25 feet below. Swimming along upside down or even snapping off an occasional barrel roll on the way down, the thoughts of ending up an early morning snack for some undersea consumer were far out of mind.

Then it happened.

On one of my more ambitious runs for the bottom, I leveled out about twenty feet down. Something was different this time, as I noticed that a good number of the fish that usually hung around had cleared out. As I looked ahead, my eyes fixed on a large stalk of kelp that towered toward the surface about fifteen feet away. Suddenly from behind the plant came my worst nightmare. Cutting a smooth but sharp arc in my direction was the leading character in a number of my least loved nightmares, a blue shark. Although it was only about five feet long, the rush of adrenaline that hit my system made the creature take on all the charming qualities of Jaws himself. The shark saw me, and being nearly as panicked as I was, angled sharply in front of me and darted away.

As the shark moved off into the murk I realized I now had a real problem. Fear had caused a surge of adrenaline to shoot through my system. The "fight or flight" reaction that had jolted every muscle in my body to attention, had also caused me to blow my entire air supply straight out of my mouth. I suddenly found myself looking above my head for an opening in the dense, fanned out kelp canopy that spread out above me. Forgetting all the wise and well worn clichés about having nothing to fear but fear itself, I began an all out kick for the surface —without a breath of air.

As I broke through the kelp canopy with all the grace and professionalism of Larry, Moe or Curley in a wet suit, coughing and gasping for oxygen at the same time, I came to realize what a formidable obstacle even 20 feet of water could be.

If a mere twenty feet of water leaves us feeling claustrophobic and more than slightly overmatched, imagine suddenly finding yourself on the sandy bottom of the Mariana Trench, the deepest point in the Pacific Ocean. As you took a look around, it might dawn on you that above your head, through the inky blackness, some 35,840 feet worth of water away is the surface. You wouldn't have long to let that thought sink in, because the immense pressure created by the weight of over six miles of water would squash you like a bug on a windshield.

The intimidating reality of dealing with water can clue us into a deeper truth. Isaiah tells us that even as overwhelming as the ocean depths can be to us, they are next to nothing to God. He is able to hold all the water of all the oceans of the world in the mere hollow of His hand. All the water in all the oceans, lakes, rivers, seas (and even back yard wading pools) combined is but a drop in the bucket to Him.

A Game of Inches?

But Isaiah tells us there is another quantum leap we must make to try to comprehend the infinity of being that is God. He tells us that God has "marked off the heavens by the span."

The art of measurement has always been a preoccupation of man. From the amateur interior decorator trying to eyeball whether that velvet Elvis painting was really centered over the sofa to the scientist measuring out spacing by nanometers (0.0000000397th of an inch) we take great pains to get an accurate grasp on distances. In the ancient near east, early carpenters, contractors and engineers would often have to settle for parceling out space by the "span," or the distance between a man's outstretched thumb and little finger.

Using that same image, Isaiah confronts us with a vision of reality that can send our imaginations reeling. Astronomers tell us that the known universe is an incredibly vast piece of real estate. In fact, if we were able to travel at the speed of light, some 186,000 miles per second, it would take us between 16 and 20 billion years to get from one end to another (not counting stops at intergalactic fast food restaurants, historical markers and tourist traps). If technology should ever rise to the level where travel at light speed were possible, and if genetic engineering would allow us to expand the length of human life to an unimaginable length of billions of years, and if we were to combine these achievements and embark on an interstellar trip from one end of the universe to the other, when we were done we would have simply traveled the distance between God's thumb and little finger.

Time Out for Some Perspective

There are certain experiences in life that remind us of our place in the grand scheme of things. Perhaps it was out on a camping trip as we stared at the awesome beauty of the soft white swath of the Milky Way and knew in our hearts we just couldn't take it all in. Perhaps it was standing on a windswept beach as we watched the shattering force of storm driven waves and gave thanks we were safely on shore. Perhaps it was the overwhelming sense of emotion and wonder that grabbed our souls as we witnessed a child being born into the world.

Experiences like these are so strangely revealing. We feel an odd mixture of being drawn to the joy and beauty of the moment, yet confronted with the strange sense of being so totally in over our heads that we almost want to turn away. Yet even these highlight moments of human existence are but a tiny inkling of the incomprehensible goodness, power and awesome majesty of God.

Staring at the Sun

It's been said that there are two great tragedies in life–not getting what you want and getting it. Could you imagine what would happen if God suddenly met the skeptic's demand and revealed himself to us completely, totally, without holding back a flicker of his radiance? In his book *Disappointment with God*, writer Philip Yancy puts this unsettling possibility into sharp focus.

Once, as an experiment, the great scientist Isaac Newton stared at the image of the sun reflected in a mirror. The brightness burned into his retina, and he suffered temporary blindness. Even after he hid for three days behind closed shutters, still the bright spot would not fade from his vision. "I used all means to divert my imagination from the sun," he writes, "but if I thought upon him I presently saw his picture though I was in the dark." If he had stared a few minutes longer, Newton might have permanently lost all vision. The chemical receptors that govern eyesight cannot withstand the full force of unfiltered sunlight. There is a parable in Isaac Newton's experiment...If you can barely endure candlelight,   how can you gaze at the sun? "Who of us can dwell with the consuming fire?" asked the prophet Isaiah. Is it possible that we should be grateful for God's hiddenness, rather than disappointed?"

The Meaning of Faith

Because of who God is, he is awfully tough to fit under a microscope or into a specimen tank. Although science can tell us quite a bit about God's creation, the Creator himself stands apart, unreachable by scientific method.

So if pure science comes up short, there a way to settle our question? Can we determine once and for all whether God really exists?

There is a way, but most people find it a bit frustrating. In the book of Hebrews this key to ultimate reality is described.

> *Now faith is the assurance of things hoped for, the conviction of things not seen...And without faith it is impossible to please Him, for he who comes to God must believe that He is, and that He is a rewarder of those who seek Him.* (Hebrews 11:1,6)

Give Me a Break

Don't tell me, let me guess. Running through your mind right now is something like, "Oh, great. Here we go again. Science can't bring us to God, so just believe. Check your intellect with the church usher on the way in. Put your brain in the offering plate as it goes by. Find a nice comfortable place to stick your head in the sand and just have faith!"

This can be a standard response for some people when they hear the dreaded word "faith." But before we close our minds to this concept we need to ask a very simple, yet crucial question. Have we ever taken the time to understand what real faith is all about?

Webster's defines faith as "allegiance or duty to a person... confidence or trust." The Bible fleshes this out by calling faith "the evidence of things not seen." Interestingly, when we start to understand faith, we begin to see it not so much as an extra added luxury option for the spiritually minded. The fact is, faith is a rock solid necessity in the day to day lives of all people.

The Dreaded Dot Test

Did you ever stop to think of how essential faith is? First of all, everyone on planet earth from Hugh Hefner to Jerry Falwell lives by faith. It is not overstating the case to say that none of us can get through one minute of the day without putting confidence in things we can't see, touch or understand completely.

A few years back I decided that I just wasn't getting enough abuse in life, so I decided to earn big money in my spare time as a high school youth director. Part of the job description (right underneath the provision about listening patiently to hour long stories of complexion breakdowns and prom night disasters) included driving an un–air–conditioned school bus crammed full of hormone crazed teenagers through the steamiest, muggiest, most boring stretch of highway in the continental United States in mid July for summer camp. In order to be state approved for such terminally insane behavior, I had to go down to the Department of Motor Vehicles and get my bus driver's license. After filling out forms that qualified me to fill out other forms and stand in lines faintly reminiscent of the wait for "Space Mountain" during Spring break, I was finally told that I could have the state's blessing as a junior Ralph Kramden if I would go and get a complete physical first. "Make an appointment with your doctor, have him fill out several thousand forms, stand in line for another three hours and you'll be all set," the bored–silly bureaucrat behind the counter monotoned.

Since the average bus driver I had encountered in life had the physique of a large Bartlett pear, I assumed that I would whiz through the physical with no problems at all. And so I did until the nurse announced there was just one more test. She handed me a book with circles filled with colored dots on each page and asked me to tell her which numbers I was able to see.

"Numbers? No problem! Let's see, there's a 5..12..15...47..22..and 86." I smiled, confidently closed the book and handed it back to her.

I knew something was up when she gave me a funny look and said, "You're kidding, right?"

"Uh, no. There's a 5..12..15...47..22 and an 86."

"So who dresses you in the morning anyway? You have to be the most color blind person I've ever tested!"

I thought about sharing with her how much I appreciated the role of sarcasm in the medical profession (i.e., "People with horned rimmed glasses and beehive hairdoos shouldn't question the fashion sense of others."), but it was all over any way. I had flunked my bus driver's physical. On the positive, this was enough to keep me from being vibrated to death piloting a bright yellow, shock absorberless tin can up Interstate 5. But there was something disturbing about the idea of going through life missing out on a good part of the visual spectrum. Add to this the fascinated reaction of those not similarly afflicted ("Color blind? Hey, what color is that red light to you?") and being color blind is simply no fun at all.

Faith Blind?

If the notion of being color blind seems strange, could you imagine what it would be like to be suddenly struck "faith blind"? What would life be like if we were unable to have trust or confidence in the unseen?

First of all, we couldn't get out of bed in the morning. After all, who is to say that the invisible force called gravity that we counted on to hold us on the planet will still be in effect in the morning? Just to be safe we would have to nail our bed posts to the floor, install seat belts on our mattress and a driver's side air bag on the ceiling just for good measure. We can't see, feel or even understand gravity completely, so why put our trust in it?

Breakfast would be a pretty iffy proposition as well. Unless we personally supervised every step of the production process, how do we know what's really in that Egg n' Cheese sandwich? What if that secret sauce contained a few extra unadvertised ingredients?

As the full implications of being faith blind began to register, our paranoia would begin to grow. I can't see, measure or weigh out character on a scientific basis, so how can I know if even my closest loved one, so seemingly warm, supportive and accepting one moment wouldn't change into Charlie Manson the next? And while we're at it, unless you live in Los Angeles you can't see air, so why let the stuff in your body? Without the ability to exercise faith we would soon find ourselves pathetic, strapped in, emaciated, isolated wretches turning blue because we were frightened even to take our next breath. The fact is, each of us exercise faith on a moment by moment basis. Whether we want to admit it or not, faith is not some impractical diversion for the spiritually minded. It is an absolute essential for living.

The Facts of Faith–Part 2

A second fact of faith is equally crucial for us to grasp, especially in a society that prides itself on tolerance of any and every perspective on reality. Faith is only as good as its object. No matter how intense my level of belief, reality has this obnoxious habit of staying constant. No matter how much emotional energy I might invest in wishing something were true, my faith is vain if it is invested in the wrong place.

This principle was driven home to me in my first adventure with the shop–by–mail industry. One day while I was browsing through the ad section of my favorite comic book, a particular offer seemed to leap off the page and catch my eye. Right below the standard "Decal–o–mania!" and "Amazing Live Sea Monkey" sales pitches was an offer so good I could hardly believe my seventh grade eyes.

Amazing Life Sized Ghost!!!

Remote controlled wonder hovers! Dances! Floats and hides again! Scare and amaze your friends! Send $2.95 to John Doe Productions, P.O. Box 100 Open Trench, Florida.

"Remote control?," I thought to myself. "This must be like one of those radio controlled airplanes! Wow! How cool to be flying my own life sized ghost around the neighborhood!"

So, with visions of creative juvenile delinquency dancing in my head, I worked feverishly pulling weeds and mowing the lawn until I had my hard earned $2.95 in hand. Since there is no zeal like that of the newly converted, I shared the good news of the life sized ghost with my good buddy, Tom. He seemed a bit skeptical about the price tag on this high tech wonder.

"This seems really cheap for a flying radio controlled ghost..."

"Oh, come on. What else could remote controlled mean? Besides, they couldn't print the ad if it wasn't on the level."

Since we were young and stupid and had never even heard of the Better Business Bureau or Ralph Nader, that logic carried the day. We sent our hard earned cash to John Doe and anxiously began our wait for the huge, elaborate UPS delivery that would begin our reign of simulated supernatural terror.

Some six weeks later, I came in the door from another mind numbingly boring day of school. As I made my way to the kitchen for my traditional post algebra headache cure (a Ding–Dong with a strong milk chaser) my Mom mentioned almost in passing that I had gotten some mail that day.

"Alright!! My Amazing Life-Sized Ghost has arrived!!! Where is it? Did they have to leave it on the back patio?"

"Uh, no." Mom replied, "In fact here it is..."

She handed me a small manila envelope with John Doe Productions scrawled out as the return address.

"Oh," I thought to myself, "Probably just a complicated set of instructions or something. The Ghost will probably come tomorrow."

But, much to my chagrin, this was it. The Amazing Life Sized Ghost turned out to be a white plastic sheet with a balloon for a head. The "remote control" was a 50 foot piece of fishing line. As I stared helplessly at the sappy, cross–eyed expression on the face of my ghost, I realized in a sickening flash that I had been taken.

Although Tom and I managed to scare the living daylights out of a mail man making his late afternoon rounds with this cheesy set up, I learned a tough lesson the hard way. No matter how sincerely I believed that this comic book offer was a high–tech marvel, it didn't change the fact that in reality it was a low–tech joke. No matter what our level of sincerity, our faith is only as good as the object we choose to invest it in.

The Ultimate Reality Check
Clearly, we all have to live with unseen reality on a day by day basis. This is an arrangement that few of us have problems accepting. We believe that wind exists, not because we see it, but because we see and feel what it does (especially if we are wearing contact lenses in Arizona). We believe that gravity exists, not because we see it, but because the first time we tried to make that 90 degree turn coming down "Deadman's Hill" on our new skateboard we became convinced that it applied to us as well.

So if everyone has faith, but faith is only as good as its object, is it reasonable for us to put our faith in God?

Just like we believe in the wind.

Just like we believe in gravity.

Not because we see God, but because he has unmistakably made His presence known in what He has done.

Take a Look Around

When we take a moment to consider the reality of the world we live in, it is important to ask a simple yet eye opening question. Do we find ourselves living in a universe of inconsistent randomness and disorder, or are we confronted with amazing intricacy and design? In his best selling book *Cosmos*, even the brilliant avowed agnostic Carl Sagan concedes;

> *Our ancestors looked at the elegance of life on Earth, at how appropriate the structures of organisms are to their functions, and saw evidence for a Great Designer...The idea that every organism was meticulously constructed by a Great Designer provided a significance and order to nature and an importance to human beings that we crave still. A Designer is a natural, appealing and altogether human explanation of the biological world.*

The View from Mount Timex

To put this another way, I would like to tell you the story of my amazing miracle watch. You see, billions and billions of years ago a huge volcano named Mount Timex blew up. From deep within the bowels of the Earth metals and elements like copper, tin and stainless steel were cast high into the primordial atmosphere and happened to impact in just the right combination. Lo and behold, this blob of molten metal happened to hit a prehistoric cow, stripping and tanning it's skin into a leather wrist band. Ages of erosion and exposure to the elements eventually resulted in what I have on my left arm today– a battery powered, day and date, alarm chronograph, water resistant to 100 meters. Now, some people used to be so silly and simplistic as to believe that a being of intelligence called a "watch maker" put this thing together, but now we know that it all can be explained by natural process, without purpose.

If you believe that, I have a number of lovely bridges you might be interested in purchasing. The nature of our universe, infinitely more complex than a simple wrist watch, shows design, purpose, and intelligence. In short, external reality demands a Creator. Granted, we can't see that Creator, but we can certainly see what He has done.

Take a Look Within

When you hear the word "craving" what kind of images come to mind? We can easily visualize harried expectant fathers in bathrobe and jammies making their way to the local all night convenience mart for pickles and ice cream. But there is another kind of craving that is part and parcel of human existence, a hunger that literally dogs our steps each and every day of our lives. It seems that an unavoidable part of being human is to have a constant need for a sense of meaning and purpose in our lives. It's been said a man can live for months without food, days without water, minutes without air, but not a single second without the conviction that somehow his life matters. In his excellent book *Kingdoms in Conflict*, former White House aide Chuck Colson stunningly illustrates this truth.

"The great Russian novelist Fyodor Dostoyevski said that not to believe in God was to be condemned to a senseless universe. In *The House of the Dead* he wrote that if one wanted to utterly crush a man, one need only give him work of a completely irrational character, as the writer himself had discovered during his ten years of prison. 'If he had to move a heap of earth from one place to another and back again – I believe the convict would hang himself... preferring rather to die than endure... such humiliation, shame and torture.'"

Some of Hitler's henchmen at a Nazi concentration camp in Hungary must have read Dostoyevski. There, hundreds of Jewish prisoners survived in disease infested barracks on little food and gruesome, backbreaking work. Each day the prisoners were marched to the compound's giant factory, where tons of human waste and garbage were distilled into alcohol to be used as a fuel additive.

Even worse than the nauseating odor of stewing sludge was the realization that they were fueling the Nazi war machine.

Then one day Allied aircraft blasted the area and destroyed the hated factory. The next morning several hundred inmates were herded to one end of its charred remains. Expecting orders to begin rebuilding, they were startled when the Nazi officer commanded them to shovel sand into carts and drag it to the other end of the plant.

The next day the process was repeated in reverse; they were ordered to move the huge pile of sand back to the other end of the compound. *A mistake has been made*, they thought. *Stupid Swine.* Day after day they hauled the same pile of sand from one end of the camp to the other.

And then Dostoyevski's prediction came true. One old man began crying uncontrollably; the guards hauled him away. Another screamed until he was beaten into silence. Then a young man who had survived three years in the camp darted away from the group. The guards shouted for him to stop as he ran toward the electrified fence. The other prisoners cried out, but it was too late; there was a blinding flash and a terrible sizzling noise as smoke puffed from his smouldering flesh.

In the days that followed, dozens of prisoners went mad and ran from their work, only to be shot by the guards or electrocuted by the fence. The commandant smugly remarked that there would soon be "no more need to use the crematoria." The gruesome lesson is plain: Men will cling to life with dogged resolve while working meaningfully, even if that work supports their hated captors. But purposeless labor soon snaps the mind. You might argue that our need to work was acquired over centuries of evolution. But we must do more than work just to survive; we must do work that has a purpose. Evolution can not explain this. More plausible is the belief of Jews and Christians that man is a reflection of the nature of a purposeful creator.

Fear and the Frozen Food Department

But there is more to the human soul than a simple need for a sense of personal significance. We also have an inescapable need to be cared for. Remember the first time you got lost in the grocery store? Everything seemed o.k. at first. As Mom made her rounds, we found display tables to hide under and carts to grab a ride on, but the real highlight of the trip was the run down the aisle that included the toy department. Dazzled by a literal treasure trove of earthly delights, every other part of reality seemed to fade away, including the fact that Mom was continuing to head for the frozen food section. After a while the collection of squirt guns, giant soap bubble kits and balsa wood gliders would begin to lose its magnetic hold on us, and suddenly we would realize that we were quite alone. Oh, to be sure there were a number of other adult like individuals wandering by, but that familiar face, the one that smiled while putting the Bactine on skinned knees, and made our special favorite dessert was no where to be found. As panic welled up within our hearts we did the only thing we knew that could possibly save the day. We threw back our heads, summoned all of our vast six year old lung power, and belted out, "MOMMMM!!!" loud enough to register on the Richter Scale at Cal Tech. Mom would poke her head around the corner of the row and our brief encounter with abandonment would fade into a tiny corner of our memory.

And yet, as we grow older, that same panic striken feeling has an obnoxious way of coming back to us. Something inside keeps bringing up a feeling that we are alone, somehow separated from someone greater than we are. Someone who loves us, whose presence will somehow go a long way toward making everything all right. As committed atheist Bertrand Russell once wrote,

> *One is a ghost, floating through the world without any real contact. Even when one feels nearest to other people, something in one seems obstinately to belong to God, and to*

refuse to enter into any earthly communion--at least that's how I should express it if I thought there was a god. It's odd, isn't it? I care passionately for this world and many things and people in it, and yet...what is it all? There must be something more important, one feels, though I don't believe there is.

How strange and ironic for people like us who supposedly live in a cold, impersonal and essentially meaningless universe to somehow have picked up the instinctive needs for purpose (which is an illusion) and connection to a Creator (who does not exist). Or could it possibly be that these traits are an unavoidably obvious set of divine finger prints, indelibly impressed upon our souls?

Take a Look Back

But perhaps the most compelling evidence that God is far more than fairy tale isn't to be found in the annals of science or psychology, but in the pages of human history.

Some who have wrestled with the question of the existence of God have turned to the Bible, believing that it would contain a full blown defense of the reality of a supreme being. Interestingly, the Bible never argues for the existence of God. In fact, the Bible calmly states that God is not hiding from us. He has not been subtle about His existence. In fact He has offered us ultimate proof by taking on humanity in the person of Jesus Christ.

Nearly 2,000 years ago a puzzled truth seeker named Philip asked a question as contemporary as tomorrow's newspaper. Turning to Jesus, exasperated and confused he said, "Lord, show us the Father, and it is enough for us."

How many of us, at our wits end from this confusing jumble of joy and pain, heart pounding crisis and mind numbing routine we call life have looked to heaven and said the same thing? "Just one sign, Lord. Just one signal from You that life isn't some pointless joke is all I'm asking. Please show me that You're real and that some how You're paying attention to an insignificant speck of dust like me."

And we wait for a reply.

We're not even sure what we're waiting for, but we wait anyway.

Philip waited too. We don't know how long it took Jesus to reply, but it was undoubtedly a charged moment. The silence was so thick you could cut it with a knife.

Some disciples probably winced, hardly believing Philip could be so rude as to make such an "un–disciple–like" request. Others grudgingly admired his courage and were secretly glad that someone had the guts to ask the question their own insecurities kept locked tight within them.

Jesus turned to Philip, probably looking more mildly surprised than irritated and said, "Have I been so long with you, and yet you have not come to know Me, Philip? He who has seen Me has seen the Father; how do you say, 'Show us the Father'? Do you not believe that I am in the Father, and the Father is in Me? The words that I say to you I do not speak on my own initiative, but the Father abiding in Me does His works. Believe Me that I am in the Father, and the Father in Me; otherwise believe on account of the works themselves" (John 14:10–11).

Philip and the others gathered there were undoubtedly stunned by this shocking reply. The challenge on the table was very simple and direct. "Show us God and settle this whole thing once and for all!"

Jesus' reply was equal to the question. "If you want to see God, look at My life."

This brief first century question and answer session raises an issue that any honest seeker of ultimate truth would do well to consider. If God did become a man, what would we expect Him to be like? We might expect to see Him make an unusual entrance into this life, to demonstrate a character completely free from any sin, to supernaturally intervene in the lives of people, to speak the most memorable words ever recorded, to exercise power over death and to make a lasting and universal impact on humanity.

How interesting to see all of these characteristics so unsubtly manifested in the life of Jesus Christ. As the famous essay, "One Solitary Life" expressed it;

> *Here is a man who was born in an obscure village, the child of a peasant woman. He grew up in another village. He worked in a carpenter's shop until He was thirty, and then for another three years He was an itinerant preacher. He never owned a home. He never wrote a book. He never held an office. He never had a family. He never went to college. He never put his foot inside a big city. He never traveled two hundred miles from the place where He was born. He never did one of the things that usually accompany greatness. He had no credentials but Himself...While still a young man, the tide of popular opinion turned against Him. His friends ran away. One of them denied Him. He was He was nailed upon a cross between two thieves. While He was dying His executers gambled for the only piece of property He had on earth–His coat. When He was dead, He was taken down and laid in a borrowed grave through the pity of a friend. Nineteen long centuries have come and gone, and today He is the centerpiece of the human race and the leader of the column of progress. I am far within the mark when I say that all the armies that ever marched, all the navies that ever were built; all the parliaments that ever sat and all the kings that ever reigned, put together, have not effected the life of man upon this earth as powerfully as has that one solitary life.*

It has been said that we are a "visited planet." God was so concerned for each of us, He settled the question of His existence once and for all by literally walking among us in the person of Jesus Christ.

Of Mice and Men

Does God exist? Is there more to Him than fantasy and sanctified fairy tale? The evidence is there for those who wish to consider it. Sometimes I am asked, if the evidence for God's existence is so overwhelming, so open and shut, why do so many intelligent people seem to reject Him?

The problem may not lie in a lack of evidence, but in how we choose to deal with the not so subtle clues God has left all around us.

There is a story that appeared in The London Observer that illustrates the frailty of our understanding. A family of mice lived in a grand piano. They enjoyed listening to the music that came from the great player who they never saw, but who they believed in, because they enjoyed the music from the piano.

One day one of the little mice got especially brave. He climbed deep into the bowels of the piano. He made an astonishing discovery. The music did not come from a great player; rather the music came from wires that reverberated back and forth. The little mouse returned to his family tremendously excited. He informed his family that there was no great player who made the piano music; rather, there were these little wires that reverberated back and forth. The family of mice abandoned their belief in a great piano player. Instead they had a totally mechanistic view.

One day one of the little mice got especially brave. He climbed even further up into the bowels of the piano. To his amazement he found that indeed the music did not come from the reverberating wires, but rather from little hammers that struck the wires. It was those hammers that really made the music. He returned to his family with a new description of the source of the music. The family of mice rejoiced that they were so educated that they understood that there was no great piano player but that the music came from little hammers that struck the wires.

The family of mice did not believe that there was a player playing the piano. Instead they believed that their mechanistic understanding of the universe explained all of reality. But the fact is that the player continued to play his music.

The question remains, are we really listening?

Discussion   Questions

1. Read through Hebrews 11. Which of the people we meet in this passage do you think faced the toughest obstacles to believing in God? Why?

2. A friend shares with you, "If God would appear in the sky for me tonight I would believe in Him." How would you respond?

3. Share a time in your life when you felt most certain that God was real. What was it about your experience you found most convincing?

4. Read Matthew 12:38–42. Why does Jesus react so strongly to this request? If God wants us to believe in Him, why doesn't He perform more miraculous signs to win us over?

CHAPTER III

NOTHING CREATED EVERYTHING

*Science commits suicide when it adopts a
creed.*

— Thomas Henry Huxley —

THE IMAGE couldn't help but grab national attention. There, in the middle of a frozen, wind swept plain of solid ice, were three personalities that soon captured the imagination of the world.

Three young California Gray Whales had stayed a bit too long in their summer feeding grounds off Point Barrow, Alaska. The frigid Arctic waters had solidified into an impenetrable barrier of thick and jagged ice, effectively cutting off the air breathing mammals from the freedom of the open sea. Network television relayed the image of three pathetic baranacle encrusted heads, gulping air through a small hole in the ice, close enough for the Eskimo Indians who discovered them to reach out and touch. Even the most hard bitten and cynical found it tough to watch these incredible creatures, bravely fighting a losing battle for survival without having the heart strings touched a bit. In fact, the amazing outpouring of sympathy and concern for the plight of the whales touched off one of the largest rescue efforts in modern memory.

Industrial size helicopters were flown in to drop huge weights on to the ice pack. Chain saws, ice choppers, and even a Soviet ice breaking ship arrived on the scene. A number of corporations volunteered to build huge nets to airlift the animals out if all else failed.

Eight days into the crisis things looked grim. The youngest whale began struggling to rise for air and eventually disappeared. There was nothing left to do but to cut a series of air holes leading to the open sea and hope that the whales' legendary intelligence would lead them to safety. In a rare example of inter–species cooperation, the plan worked. On day fifteen the two survivors successfully escaped their icy prison. Television viewers all over the world breathed a sigh of relief.

What is it about these tremendous sea creatures that so instantly grabs our attention? As *U.S. News and World Report* summed it up;

> *Nothing like them in the world's imagination. Associated with ferocity in the Bible; with enormity by Milton; with government by Hobbes's Leviathan; with prehistoric power by Melville: "He swam the seas before the continents broke water." The Anglo-Saxons called the oceans "whale roads" in deference to the animal's dominion. A whale rescued Jonah, one of our own. Point Barrow offered the chance to return the favor.*

There is no doubt about the fact that whales are amazing. Consider that the Blue Whale, at over 100 feet in length, weighs more than 2,500 people. It's tongue alone is ten feet thick and is heavier than an elephant. It's arteries are large enough for a child to swim through, and yet for all it's massive size the Blue can travel at speeds over 15 knots, generating up to 1,000 horsepower.

Humpbacks are powerful enough to heave their 40 ton bodies completely out of the water. They also have devised an incredibly efficient feeding technique called "bubble netting." Rapidly circling under a school of fish, the whale forces bursts of air through its blowhole, creating a rising spiral of bubbles that acts as a corral. Instantly the whale will burst up from underneath, gulping down several hundred pounds of fish at once.

Killer whales hunt in extremely organized packs, even using bursts of high frequency sound waves to stun fleeing salmon. And we haven't even begun to mention the whale's built in sonar or the sophisticated ability to communicate with others of its species hundreds of miles away.

An Amazing Story

Have you ever stopped to wonder how these amazing creatures came to be? Consider this popular explanation offered in *Readers Digest* Magazine.

> *Most authorities believe that 60 million years ago ancestors of modern whales were four legged, wolf-size animals living on the shores of estuaries and lagoons, where an abundance of fish and shrimp enticed them to try wading. As nature favored those best equipped for swimming, evolution began reshaping them. Over 10 to 15 million years, their bodies grew, forelegs shrank into flippers used for balance and steering, and hind legs disappeared. To propel themselves through the water, whales grew tapered tales ending in horizontal, paddle like flukes. The nose in most species moved to the top of the head and became separated from the mouth; whales could therefore feed without filling their lungs with sea water and breathe without sticking their heads up. The insides were restructured, too, so whales could move, feed and communicate entirely underwater. As a result of these amazing transformations, they are now helpless on land. If stranded on a beach, they can hardly breathe.*

At the risk of offending the white lab coat set, we need to ask ourselves a simple question. Does the idea of one of the most perfectly well suited creatures to live in the sea originating when a wolf–like animal developed a taste for sushi make sense?

Or could there be a better explanation, not only for whales with built–in sonar, but for the geometrically precise architecture of bees, the navigational abilities of migrating birds, and the ability of human beings to even ask such questions? Is life as we know it the result of choice and planning by an intelligent Designer, or merely the outcome of a series of lucky breaks? The controversy rages all around us today.

In the Beginning

Perhaps the best first step toward gaining clarity in any debate is to understand the basic position of both sides of the issue. After a lifetime of Star Trek episodes and classroom slide presentations most of us are familiar with the nuts and bolts of the evolutionist perspective of our origins. Evolution teaches that the universe we live in is a self–sufficient place where self contained physical laws develop everything into higher levels of order and complexity. Particles work their way into elements, elements transform into complex chemicals, complex chemicals into simple living organisms, simple life forms to the more complex, and finally complex animal life developed into man.

The driving, directing force behind this process is mathematical probability. In the words of Nobel Prize winning molecular biologist Jaques Monod, "Chance alone is at the source of every innovation, of all creation in the biosphere. Pure chance, absolutely free but blind, is at the very root of the stupendous edifice of evolution."

There is, however a differing view of origins called creationism. Creationists hold that all reality we experience today emerged from a specific time of God's creative activity at the beginning of time. During this period of special creation all the basic laws and categories of nature were brought into being by processes which are no longer operating today. In other words, no new species are coming into existence at this time. Once the creation was finished, the processes of creation were replaced by systems of conservation designed to sustain and maintain the basic systems already in place.

Creationists also hold that a basic principle of disintegration now dominates the universe (as anyone who has tried their hand at home improvement knows, things are breaking down rather than getting better) and that much of what is usually seen as the product of countless years of gradual process may actually be evidence of world wide catastrophies in the not too distant past.

The key to the creationist position is the existence and activity of a purposeful Creator. As the first verse of the Bible expresses it, "In the beginning God created the heavens and the earth."

And the Winner Is....

Which side of this controversy is carrying the day in our sophisticated, media saturated culture? Opinion polls conducted on college campuses and with the average man on the street show that well over 60 percent of Americans opt for an evolutionary understanding of our origins. If this were a presidential election, creationism would be hard pressed to carry a single state.

Why such a land slide victory? Certainly those in the evolutionary camp would state that the facts themselves leave any truly thinking individual little choice but to jump on the Darwinian band wagon. But the real reasons for the popularity of evolutionary thought may be more complex than what we have been lead to believe. Consider for instance, how creationism is typically represented in the media. In the early eighties the state of Arkansas passed a law allowing creationism to be taught as an alternative to evolution. The statute was immediately challenged in the courts. Chuck Colson in his excellent book, *Who Speaks for God?* offers an interesting insight into the media coverage of the issue.

Consider how the Washington Post described the parties involved: "The ACLU and the New York firm of Skadden Arps attacked the Arkansas law with a powerful case. Their brief is so good that there is talk of publishing it. Their witnesses gave brilliant little summaries of several fields of science, history and religious philosophy." Such was the "enlightened" plantiff. The creationist witnesses, however were "impassioned believers, rebellious educators and scientific oddities. All but one of the creation scientists came from obscure colleges or Bible schools. The one who didn't, said he believed diseases dropped from space, that evolution caused Nazism, and that insects may be more intelligent than humans but are hiding their abilities." It goes on. The point is simple. If you were an uninformed reader, who would you believe – the firm of Skadden Arps with its brilliant summaries, or the backwoods weirdos from no-name colleges? One can only conclude that in Arkansas in December of 1981, to question evolutionary theory – that is, to be Christian – was to be stupid. High Noon at the Laboratory.

It seems clear that the intellectual universe just ain't big enough for both theories to co–exist. As the noted French philosopher Pierre Teilhard de Chardin put it, "Evolution is a general postulate to which all theories, all hypotheses, all systems must henceforward bow and which they must satisfy in order to be thinkable and true. Evolution is a light which illuminates all facts, a trajectory which all lines of thought must follow."

One can only sit through so many classroom lectures, National Geographic television specials and B–grade science fiction movies before we can fall prey to a popular, but faulty line of reasoning:

A.   We want to be seen as educated, intelligent people.
B.   We are told that most educated, intelligent people believe in evolution.

C. We believe in evolution because we believe most
educated, intelligent people believe in evolution.

Is this reason enough to buy into an evolutionary world
view? No. No more than it is enough for a Christian to buy
into creationism because, "After all, my dear sainted
mother believes in it, and that red–faced bellowing
preacher I listen to every Sunday is absolutely convinced
about it, and every one sitting around me in church nods in
full agreement with it. It must be true!" We must be open
and honest enough to ask ourselves which of these two
views best fits the facts. Which explanation best
corresponds with reality? If either position runs into
insurmountable problems, we must have the personal
integrity to take another look at our point of view. We
must ask ourselves if our position is intellectually,
practically and personally consistent.

I'd Rather Be Lucky Than Created?

Futurist Alvin Toffler once described our society as
being "future shocked." People are bombarded with too
many choices to deal with in too short a span of time.
After a dizzying week of wrestling with burning questions
like regular or unleaded? Diet or regular? With cheese or
without? Most of us want to avoid making hard choices
like the plague. We feel much more comfortable being
perceived as moderate or even undecided. But when it
comes down to the question of how this crazy universe of
ours got going we are faced with one of those nasty
"either–or," no–middle–ground, one way or the other
situations. Outside the realm of over dramatic gangster
films there is no such thing as a "purposeful accident." We
are here either by choice or by chance with precious little
room for a nice warm moderate position in between.

Chances Are?

To be fair, both the choice and chance positions on
origins face some difficult problems. Evolution for
instance, would modify the opening line of Genesis to read,

"In the beginning, chance created the heavens and the earth..." Emminent scientists like Jaques Monod tell us that chance is the creating, sustaining, guiding agent of all things.

But there is one major problem with this commonly accepted notion. You can't walk out to get the paper one warm summer morning and find a pile of "chance" on your lawn. You can't yell at "chance" for having eleven items in the express check out line at the grocery store. You can't find a wad of "chance" stuck to your shoe after a ball game. Why? Because chance does not exist in the real world. As writer R.C. Sproul summed up:

> *That anything can happen by chance is an impossible supposition. I can readily suppose that one thing can cause another. I can conceive of God causing things, of men causing things, and of microbiological organisms causing things. But I cannot suppose of chance causing things. Why not? Because chance is not a theory. Chance is a word to describe mathematical possibilities. Chance is not an entity. It has no being. It is no thing. It is nothing. What Carl Sagan wants me to suppose is that something is caused by nothing. Here Sagan leaves both science and philosophy in the dust and indulges in untenable mythology. There is a vast difference between a God-hypothesis and the chance-hypothesis. The concept of God is a concept of a real being with real power. Chance, on the other hand, has no being and therefore no power. The bottom line in the modern myth is the idea of something out of nothing. If there is one absolute, non-negotiable, necessary idea for science and philosophy it is the law, the overarching law of nature, indeed the sina qua non (an absolutely indispensible concept)of all scientific inquiry, that ex nihilo nihil fit (out of nothing, nothing comes).*

Alchemy 101?

Clearly the idea of chance as creator leaves us with some serious problems. And yet how often have we heard our brightest and best scientific minds resort to the use of terms like "accident," "coincidence" or even "fate" to describe the chain of events that has lead to the reality we experience today? In my high school biology class I recall the teacher smirkingly telling us that there was a time when people were ignorant enough to believe in a theory called "spontaneous generation." This hay seed concept stated that life came from non life, that frogs were magically created from mud and that maggotts sprang to life from rotting meat. When asked how this amazing transformation worked, the average person would say, "We don't know, it just does. Everyone knows that." Ironically, when we ask modern science how life came into existence on the planet, they tell us that there were these non living chemicals floating in some primordial soup and that a chance burst of electricity or some other form of energy transformed them into a living creature. How exactly did this happen? We don't really know, but trust us, it did. Everyone knows that. How interesting that our modern view of the origin of life, called "abiogenesis" isn't all that far removed from "spontaneous generation." Subtract a few billion years, a sludgy sea of smelly chemicals and a lightning bolt straight out of Frankenstein from the process and we have in essence the same theory.

It Just Happened, Dad! Honest!

Has something ever come from nothing? Is there any such thing as an uncaused effect? It seems we discover from an early age that common sense argues strongly against these notions. When I was about five years old, my brother and I began to make our first ventures into the exciting world of home aerodynamics. We discovered that the tall chest of drawers in our parent's bed room was situated just close enough to the bed to provide us with about a second and a half of the thrill of free fall. While one of us would watch, either giggling uncontrollably or doing a double–time jazz version of the theme to "Batman," the other would leap spread eagle through the air on to a soon to be worn out and lumpy mattress.

From a five–year–old point of view there were few things in life that could possibly be more fun than this. Craving bigger and bigger thrills, we would try to extend the hang time on our leaps, going higher and higher and closer and closer to the ceiling until...

BANG!!!

The Sears Best metal bed frame just couldn't take the shock any longer. The mattress, once so level and run way–like would end up sticking up in the air like some kind of monsterous, sheet and comforter covered ice berg. Panic seized, we would leap into action, desperately trying to get the frame straightened out and the box spring back in place.

Then the bedroom door would swing open. The figure of a large, displeased parent would fill the door way.

"What did I tell you about jumping on the bed?"

"Oh Dad, really we weren't jumping on the bed. We just walked into the room and the thing fell apart!"

"Yeah, Dad. It was the weirdest thing I've ever seen. It just happened. Kind of like the Twilight Zone or something!"

Like any other parent, my Dad was unconvinced that the laws of nature had been mysteriously suspended in a small bed room in Canoga Park, California. This effect (a broken bed) definitely had a cause (two hyperactive juveniles). I doubt if he would have been any more impressed if we had try to pawn our misdeeds off on random selection, blind chance or fate.

The fact that an uncaused effect has never been demonstrated presents a huge problem for those that claim that life "simply happened." Evolutionary explanations of reality run into a serious obstacle at this point.

Talk Show Theology

It's been said that there are three key warning signs that allow you to know that you're well on your way to becoming the same kind of old fuddy duddy that used to drive you crazy during your obnoxious teen years. If you find yourself complaining about the pathetic state of the music "these kids today" enjoy, or beginning any story with the words, "When I was your age...," or find yourself more and more attracted to AM radio, chances are you're getting nearer and nearer to old coot status. I have to confess that more than once on a late night trip home from a speaking engagement I have found myself strangely drawn away from the "heavy hits" to the wild and wacky world of the late night AM talk show. One such evening I tuned into a nationally syndicated program and caught the host engaging in a little amature theology. After cutting off a well intentioned religious zealot, he paused meaningfully and observed, "You know, I hear these people going on and on about how God created everything, but no one's ever been able to answer this one for me. Who created God?"

Between a Rock and a Hard Place

Usually a question like this has a funny way of being less of a question than a quick and easy way to put a heavy lid on a pot of conversation whose brew might not suit our taste. Rather than explore spiritual issues in an open and meaningful way, it's much more simple to launch a rhetorical Scud missle (like "Can God make a rock so big that He can't lift it?") and move on to more important matters (like "I wonder if that rabbit should be allowed to have a bowl of Trix after all?"). But interestingly, this kind of verbal roadblock raises a very legitimate issue. Does the principle that it is impossible for something to come from nothing apply to God as well?

To answer this question we first need to understand that the idea of a self–existent, uncaused being is not irrational. Classical philosophers like Aristotle saw the idea of an "unmoved–mover" as the basis of understanding reality. Secondly, when we ask the question "Who created God?" we may find ourselves falling into the trap of being like the proverbial Ugly American tourist who insists that everything in the place he visits be just like home.

Our home turf is a reality governed by time. From the alarm clock that rattles our sleep saturated brains every Monday morning to the moment we suddenly realize the bratty little squirt we used to tease at the bus stop is now six–foot–five (and is contemplating revenge), we are surrounded with reminders that time is always on the move. It is a given that people are born, grow old and die. All things seem to have a beginning and an end. But is this the case with God? The Bible describes God as being the One who "was, is and is to come," that He is "everlasting," and "is the same yesterday, today and forever." The clear message of Scripture is that God is not bound by time. In fact, He exists in a timeless state some have called the eternal now, and therefore has no need of a creator. As God Himself bluntly put it:

> *You are My witnesses and the servant whom I have chosen, in order that you may know and believe Me, and understand that I am He. Before Me there was no God formed, and there will be none after Me.* (Isaiah 43:10)

Is it difficult to conceive of timelessness? We might as well ask a fish who lives five miles below the surface if it's easy to conceive of sunlight. But our difficulty in understanding the concept does not change reality one single bit. God Himself is the author of all reality. He has always been.

Meanwhile, Back in the Real World

Although the evolutionary perspective on reality states that all things came into existence by a non–existent set of mathematical probabilities called chance, and the creationist point of view tells us that a real being called God purposefully made all things, both sides agree on one proposition. Ours is a marvelously complex universe, awe inspiring in the design and intricacy of even the smallest, simplest things. But does this evidence of order and intelligence in the creation point to a master designer?

In his book, *Evolution: A Theory In Crisis*, Austrailian biologist and agnostic Michael Denton asked,

Is it really credible that random processes could have constructed a reality, the smallest element of which– a functional protein or gene– is complex beyond our own creative capacities, a reality which is the very antithesis of chance, which excels in every sense anything produced by the intelligence of man?

Renowned evolutionist Carl Sagan would answer, "Yes!" In his best selling book, *Cosmos*, Sagan poetically observes;

A Designer is a natural, appealing and altogether human explanation of the biological world. But as Darwin and Wallace showed, there is another way, equally appealing, equally human and far more compelling; natural selection, which makes the music of life more beautiful as the aeons pass.

The message? Sure, there is beauty, intricacy, an inimitable level of design easily apparent in the universe. And isn't it even more amazing that its all just a big accident? Amazing wouldn't be the word for it. Try incredible. Or if you'll pardon the expression, miraculous. Right up there with a tornado sweeping through a junkyard and assembling a fully functional 747 (complete with those lovely honey roasted peanuts and an in–flight movie).

This explosions–in–print–shops–make–encyclopedias
line of thought gets tougher and tougher to hold on to when
we see science more than willing to buy into a linkage of
design and designer on other controversial questions.
Commenting on Carl Sagan's *Cosmos*, R.C. Sproul observes;

> *Sagan's preference for chance, accident,
> randomness (and at one point he uses the
> word "fate"!) as more compelling than an
> ultimate Designer gets shaky when he turns his
> attention away from evolution and focuses on
> the intriguing question of life on Mars or other
> planets: "Intelligent life on Earth first reveals
> itself through the geometric regularity of its
> constructions. If Lowell's canal network really
> existed, the conclusion that intelligent beings
> inhabit Mars might be similarly compelling."
> Once again we encounter the problem of the
> missing cake. Here Sagan sees design as
> evidence of intelligent beings. He can't seem
> to rid himself entirely of the assumptions made
> by our ancestors, that order implies an
> Orderer, that design implies a Designer.*

The Bible, on the other hand, embraces the order in our
universe. In fact, it celebrates reality as a sign of the
intelligence, creativity and love of God. As the book of
Revelation so eloquently expresses it,

> *You are worthy, our Lord and God, to receive
> glory and honor and power, for You created
> all things, and by Your will they were created
> and have their being.*

The Credibility Gap

Now at this point a valid question is raised. If a
Designer based view of reality seems to make so much
sense, why aren't more scientists convinced?

Sad to say most scientists seem not only to be
unconvinced about the role of God in the creation, but have
a decidedly emotional, even angry response when the
subject comes up. A few years back I read a guest opinion
in the local newspaper concerning an upcoming seminar on

creation science. The writer, an astronomy teacher at a near by junior college, wrote of his anguish that not only were there those who believed in all this God nonsense, but had the nerve to say that their position was better supported by objective evidence than evolution. He wrote;

While you won't find any competent scientist who will accept that claim, there are plenty of laymen who find it quite acceptable. This is largely due to the fact that very little is taught in our public schools on the origins of things. How abundant is their claimed evidence? A few years ago, two scientists did a huge literature search for all claimed evidence for scientific creationism and found *absolutely nothing* in its favor in scientific journals over a three–year span in the mid–80's.

This sounds like a serious indictment until we begin to consider some key facts of life.

Heresy Hunting for Fun and Profit

If this study was accurate, why was absolutely nothing published in favor of creationism in the mid–eighties? Was there really a lack of serious writing on the subject, or was the problem to be found upstairs in editorial?

Consider the strange case of Forrest Mims III. Until recently Mims contributed articles to Scientific American magazine under a column called Amateur Scientist. His work was a series of "How–to" pieces on home chemistry or physics experiments. His columns were always free from editorial comment, well thought out and well received. Every one was happy about Forrest being a part of the Scientific American team until one day, in a conversation with the editor, he let slip that he had come to believe in the creationist theory of origins. The reaction? Mims was dropped from the magazine staff so quickly you'd need a home physics experiment to measure the speed. Plans to make Mims a regular writer for the magazine were scrapped. In exchange for a promise not to sue, Scientific American agreed to accept three more columns from him and no more. The stink that was raised nation–wide over this parting of the ways revealed a decidedly human side of the proudly unemotional world of the white lab coat and bunsen burner set. As syndicated columnist Paul Greenberg observed;

> *"Evolution is science," we are now informed by an editorial in the Arkansas Gazette, daily newspaper and scientific arbiter. "Scientists still argue over the details of the process, but there is no doubt that existing species of plants and animals evolved from earlier forms." OK, OK, no sense arguing with a dogma. But a question: If the theory of evolution ain't a theory any more, if it's science and therefore beyond doubting, why do some of its adherents exhibit the same attitudes that characterize the more perfervid defenders of other belief systems? To quote Robert Park, physicist at the University of Maryland, on the unorthodox Mims: "If he believes in creationism, he has established that he doesn't have credibility to write about science." Not since the Hollywood blacklist have a writer's ideas been cited as evidence for not letting his work appear in certain hallowed precincts. It's hard to decide whether this affair is more appalling or amusing. The sight of a writer being dropped because of thoughtcrime is not new. The delicious aspect is that he's being suppressed in the name of science, which is supposed to be above matters of faith and heresy. Of course it isn't. It only sounds that way because of the shaky modern supposition that science -unlike history or politics or government or other such "subjective" arts- is immune to the tides of fashion and belief. Any historian of science might testify otherwise. "The worst kind of science education," says one chronicler of evolution's change from theory to dogma, "is the kind that tells students it is wrong to question the pronouncements of authority." Irving Kristol put it this way- "our goal should be to have biology and evolution taught in a way that points to what we don't*

*know as well as what we do." Instead
"Scientific" American seems to have devised a
loyalty test for its writers. And an apostate like
Forrest Mims III can't pass.*

As much as our culture is loathe to admit it, science is
not something that occurs in a sanitary vacuum,
completely devoid of human foible and frailty. Scientists
are people and it seems that each human being comes
factory equipped with a particular axe to grind. Bigotry,
intolerance and zeal out of control are occupational
hazzards no matter where we hang our vocational hat–
behind a pulpit or a steering wheel or a computer terminal.
The danger comes when we lose sight of the fact that we
are as prone to create our own home version of the Spanish
Inquisition as the next person.

Has the Jury Reached a Verdict?

Our controversy raises another key question. Are all
"competent" scientists really in lock step with the
evolutionary world view? Colin Patterson, senior
paleontologist for the British Museum of Natural History,
told a group of scientists gathered at the American
Museum of Natural History in New York that belief in
evolution was just as much a commitment to faith as a
belief in a Creator. "I woke up and realized that all my life
I had been duped into taking evolutionism as revealed
truth in some way." He stated that no real transitional
forms had ever been found in the fossil record. He added,
"I don't think we shall ever have any access to any form of
the (evolutionary) tree which we can call factual." He went
on to challenge other scientists to tell him one thing they
knew as a certainty about evolution. "I tried it on members
of the Evolutionary Morphology Seminar in the University
of Chicago, a very prestigious body of evolutionists, and
all I got there was silence for a very long time and
eventually one person said, 'I do know one thing–it ought
not to be taught in high school.'"

A Man's Got To Know His Limitations

So what conclusions can we come to in the midst of a controversy that has undoubtedly generated a lot more heat than light over the years? First, the question of creation versus evolution is by definition unscientific. The theory of evolution exists outside the realm of pure science because as a process it is not repeatable, testable or verifiable. Why? Because the advent of whales and crab grass and little green apples all happened in the past, and even if the process continues it is too gradual to be observed. If we sit around watching our Siberian Husky, waiting for its nostrils to migrate to the top of its head so it can better chase ducks in the local pond, we'll be watching for quite a while.

Creationism fares no better under the definition of pure science because it too happened in the past and doesn't seem to be happening in the now. We can't for instance set up an empty fish tank and say, "OK, God how about a mini version of a self sustaining ecosystem, ex–nihilo? Ready..Set..Create!"

Is this a knock on creationism or evolutionism? No. It's simply an acknowledgement that the scientific method has its limitations. Science has profoundly positive contributions to make when it comes to making a better motor oil, or a vacine for a devestating disease or a breath spray that will improve your social life, but science in and of itself can never answer any ultimate questions. Questions like, is there really a meaning and purpose to our lives? Will I survive beyond the grave? Am I alone in this universe? Is there a God who made us and cares for us deeply?

Ironically, whatever path in this controversy we opt to follow, we will still find ourselves ending up in the same place–face to face with such ultimate questions. Consider this bit of insight from Dr. Robert Jastrow, Director of NASA's Goddard Institute for Space Studies. While

Jastrow doesn't believe in God, he eloquently describes the final destination of our modern flurry of scientific inquiry;

> ...the world had a beginning under conditions in which the known laws of physics are not valid, and as a product of forces or circumstances we cannot discover...the scientist's pursuit of the past ends in the moment of creation! For the scientist who has lived by his faith in the power of reason, the story ends like a bad dream. He has scaled the mountains of ignorance; he is about to conquer the highest peak, as he pulls himself over the final rock, he is greeted by a band of theologians who have been sitting there for centuries.

The bottom line? An external look at the creation around us eventually leads us to an inward look within our own souls. The Bible tells us that our perspective on our environment and our origins can reveal quite a bit about how we feel about its Author. As the apostle Paul expressed it,

> ...that which is known about God is evident within (humanity); for God made it evident to them. For since the creation of the world His invisible attributes, His eternal power and divine nature, have been clearly seen, being understood through what has been made, so that they are without excuse. For even though they knew God, they did not honor Him as God, or give thanks; but they became futile in their speculations, and their foolish heart was darkened. Professing themselves to be wise, they became fools.

This verse provides a glimpse into the reasons why anger and strong emotion seem to follow this issue. The question of our ultimate origin eventually makes us take a hard look at where we stand with God. If we love Him, there is little problem accepting His role as Creator. Appreciating His creation will be a constant source of joy. We will never be able to view another sunset without a warm smile and a deep sense of "Hey! I know the guy who

made that!" crossing our mind. But if we've shut God out
of our lives, we will find ourselves going to extreme lengths
to ignore Him, deny Him, and keep ourselves a safe
distance away from Him.

But God has stacked the deck against such alienation.
Another scientist, physicist Blaise Pascal observed that
within each of us there exists a "God shaped vacuum," a
void that He alone can fill. Creationism and evolutionism
are both attempts to cope with this emptiness. And
perhaps this is where we will find the most important
question we will face in this debate. Which perspective
best explains not only what we see in the universe around
us, but also the spiritual hunger within us as well?

Discussion Questions

1. Read Romans 1:18–23. Is the truth about God "suppressed" in our culture? Give an example to support your answer.

2. A friend claims that there is simply not enough evidence to support the idea of a creator behind the universe. How would you respond?

3. Do you believe a creationistic perspective of origins should be taught in public schools? Why or why not?

4. Read Psalm 19:1–6. Have you ever seen an aspect of nature that convinced you there must be a creator? Share your experience.

CHAPTER IV
TED BUNDY IS BASICALLY GOOD

*It's really a wonder I haven't dropped all my
ideals because they seem so absurd and
impossible to carry out. Yet I keep them,
because in spite of everything I still believe
that people are really good at heart.*

— Anne Frank, 1944 —

CHILDREN ARE an incredibly valuable natural source. Not only are they our hope for tomorrow, but they also possess an innate ability to reveal the truth about who we really are. A prime example of this phenomenon recently took place in an unlikely location. The world caught a glimpse of the true inner nature of mankind in Midland, Texas.

It all started innocently enough. On a warm autumn afternoon, two pre-schoolers decided to play a game "family." Going next door, they enlisted their blonde eighteen-month-old neighbor to play the time honor role of "baby." The threesome proceeded to strike out across the backyard in traditional family formation "daddy" on the right, "mommy" on the left, and "baby" in the middle.

Suddenly, something was desperately wrong. "Baby" was gone. She had fallen into the mouth of an old abandoned well partially covered by the backyard grass. Trapped some twenty feet below the rocky surface of the earth, the plight of Jessica McClure gripped the hearts of a neighborhood town, and eventually an entire nation.

Volunteers, experts in drilling, excavation and rescue techniques, swarmed in from across the country. Network news reporters recorded the round the clock efforts as a race against time and seemingly impossible circumstances kept the world on the edge of its seat.

Then, some fifty–eight hours after the ordeal began, Jessica emerged from her dark prison in the arms of a sweat–soaked, tough–as–nails rescue volunteer. The glaring camera lights revealed intense emotions, the collective sense of relief and joy shared by Jessica's parents, her neighbors, and yes, even the world.

Bob Green, syndicated columnist with the *Chicago Tribune*, spoke for many when he wrote:

> *What happened in Midland last week showed something that many of us have realized for some time now—that outside of New York and Washington and Los Angeles and the other so called "power centers" of the nation, there are still people who are willing to do something for the most elementary, yet noble reason of all: because that something is right. I write these words only minutes after Jessica McClure has been pulled from the hole. I do not know what her ultimate fate will be. By the time these words reach you, you will know much more about that than I do at this moment.*
>
> *But I know this: I am so proud of this country. I am so, so proud.*[6]

The ordeal of Jessica McClure was much more than simply an emotional suspense saga. In it we caught sight of a greater, hidden reality. A group of people were willing to lay down time, money, grueling effort, and even their own lives to save a trapped and helpless child. The story of Jessica showed us a clear picture of the ability of ordinary human beings to act with nobility, bravery, and a gritty kind of dignity when the chips were down. The plight of a helpless child can truly bring out the best in us.

Interestingly, it was that same concern for the welfare of children that motivated another somewhat organized group action in Chalmette, Louisiana. The results in this "crisis" situation were quite a bit different than the miracle in Midland.

According to the Associated Press, adults took matters into their own hands at the "Cutest Kid in the World" pageant. Contest promoter Ann Berry told reporters that due to technical difficulties, the pageant ran some four hours behind schedule on its first day. Frustration began to build in the crowded auditorium until suddenly a mother of one of the contestants climbed up on to the stage, snatched the microphone from the emcee and—at the top of her lungs—urged parents to get their money back. This seemed to be an idea whose time had come. The parents responded by storming the stage, making off with contest prizes, a computer, and a cash box with the door receipts. The "Cutest Kid" trophy, more than six feet tall, went down the center aisle with two men fighting over it. Children, it seems, can bring out the best and the worst in us.

In case you hadn't noticed, we live in a strange world. Not that the world itself is so complex; it's just the people who live in it that are tough to figure out.

Take a look at the morning paper. On the front page we can read the inspiring story of Mother Teresa calling for practical compassion for the dying and dispossessed of the third world. The next column over we can discover that a Middle Eastern head of state has put a five million dollar bounty on the life of an author of differing religious convictions. The composer of the hit song "Peace Train" (sample lyric: "Why must we go on hating? Why can't we live in bliss?") goes public with his opinion that bumping off this "infidel" is a great idea. The dignity and depravity of human nature, our glory and our shame, all there in black and white.

What are we supposed to believe about human nature?

Do we listen to the cynical and disgusted tell us that people are animals and simply "no darn good"?

Do we buy into the closed–eye optimism that tells us that people are really good at heart in a world filled with terrorism, violence, and oppression?

Or does the truth lie somewhere in between?

Is it possible to gain an accurate view of who we are as human beings? To understand ourselves as we truly are, we must answer three critical questions.

Question 1: Why Are We?

Have you ever stopped to wonder how the human race got started on planet Earth? There is no shortage of debate on this issue today. The prevalent view in our culture states that you and I, Jessica McClure, and the rowdies of Chalmette are the result of a big accident. Time, plus matter and energy, plus chance is ultimately responsible for everything from the Italian renaissance to "I Love Lucy" reruns. Nobel–Prize–winning molecular biologist Jacques Monod put it this way: "The universe was not pregnant with life, nor the biosphere with man. Our number came up in a Monte Carlo game. Is it any wonder if, like the person who has just made a million at the casino, we feel strange and a little unreal?"

Listening to public broadcasting, sitting in a university classroom, or watching a Jacques Cousteau special, we can begin to believe that the idea of man as a product of process, without purpose, is a settled issue.

Yet how difficult it is for us to reconcile this idea with real life. Gazing at the works of da Vinci, seeing the wonder in the eyes of a small child on her first trip to Disneyland, or watching an elderly couple holding hands at the bus stop makes it hard to believe that all we are is a nice roll of some chemical dice.

In contrast, the Bible emphatically states that there is far more than luck involved in the presence of man on earth.

Think through your own life experiences. What does the geology, the geography, the relentlessly consistent set of natural laws we live with day to day tell us about our world? The simple fact that our planet can support life strongly suggests that we are here by choice, not by chance.

Cosmos Revisited

To better appreciate the environment in which we live, let's use a little creativity. Imagine you are coming to take a look at our quaint solar neighborhood with Jane Jetson of Century 29 Cosmic Realty. In which neck of the woods would you like to put up your white picket fence and plastic flamingos?

You say you're a desert rat? Consider the nice dry heat of Mercury. The nighttime temperature is a comfortable seventy degrees. But when daytime rolls around be sure to pack your industrial strength sun screen. The afternoon high tops out in the low eight hundreds, hot enough to melt lead.

A little southern humidity more to your liking? Take a look at Venus. Its thick atmosphere traps heat very efficiently resulting in a surface temperature of six hundred degrees and an atmospheric pressure nearly one hundred times greater than Earth at sea level (or fifty times greater than Florida in the summertime).

More inclined to the rarefied air of the high country? Mars could be just your cup of tea. The atmosphere is 98 percent less dense than here on Earth. But on the positive side, the constant dust storms make for some striking sunsets!

Perhaps you're more used to the cosmopolitan lifestyle of the big city. You just don't trust breathing air that you can't see? Jupiter, with its delightful, swirling methane and ammonia atmosphere could be just the ticket for you.

During the hey–day of the space program, American astronauts experienced a slice of life on the stark and lifeless Moon. Consistently these men would look back at the Earth and describe it as a beautiful, fragile island of life in a cold and foreboding universe. In the words of Apollo 14 crew member Edgar Mitchell, our planet is "a sparkling blue and white jewel... laced with slowly swirling veils of white... like a small pearl in a thick sea of black mystery."[7]

Would it surprise you to learn that God was way ahead of our space program? In Isaiah 45:18 we read, "For thus says the LORD, who created the heavens (He is the God who formed the earth and made it, He established it and did not create it a waste place, But formed it to be inhabited), I am the LORD, and there is none else."

The existence of life on Earth can provide significant insight into ultimate reality. God considers humanity to be of such tremendous value He created this marvelous environment, this awesomely unique world, to support and sustain us.

Special Place—Special People

Not only is the planet we dwell on something special, the Bible states that you and I as human beings are unique as well. According to Scripture, we are creatures of incredible potential. We can think, invent, and create. Our insatiable curiosity and ingenuity have made even space travel possible. We can engage in acts of selfless compassion and mercy to one another. We are possessors of conscience and moral awareness, deeply concerned with issues of right and wrong. In Psalm 8:3–5, Israel's famous poet King David aptly summed up our place in the grand scheme of things when he said, "When I consider Thy heavens, the work of Thy [God's] fingers, / The moon and the stars, which Thou hast ordained; / What is man, that Thou dost take thought of him? / And the son of man, that Thou dost care for him? / Yet, Thou hast made him a little lower than God, / And dost crown him with glory and majesty!"

Our incredible planet and our amazing potential raise a very important question.

Why?

Why has God gone to such effort to create us and situate us and sustain us? What were we put here to do?

The answer to this age–old, ultimate question is so profound that a thousand lifetimes could not exhaust its depths, yet so simple that a child can understand it. *We are here to relate.*

You and I and every person who lives on the face of the earth are here for one common purpose: To enter into a personal relationship with the God who created us and loves us, and to relate to others as He desires.

The apostle Paul speaking to a group of first century truth seekers said, "And He made from one, every nation of mankind to live on all the face of the earth, having determined their appointed times, and the boundaries of their habitation, that they should seek God, if perhaps they might grope for Him and find Him, though He is not far from each one of us; for in Him we live and move and exist, as even some of your own poets have said, 'For we also are His offspring'" (Acts 17:26–28).

Jesus underscored the ultimate importance of relationship in a dialogue with a lawyer of His day. The lawyer asked, "Teacher, which is the great commandment in the Law?" He replied, "'You shall love the Lord your God with all your heart, and with all your soul, and with all your mind.' This is the great and foremost commandment. The second is like it, 'You shall love your neighbor as yourself.' On these two commandments depend the whole Law and the Prophets" (Matt. 22:36–40).

In Jesus' simple, yet direct reply we can glean answers to questions that have haunted the minds of humanity, from the philosopher ensconced in his academic ivory tower, to the blue collar worker relaxing on the front porch, watching the sun go down at the end of a tough day.

Why are we here? To live out a love relationship with God and humanity.

What does God ultimately ask us to do? To love God with the entirety of our being and to share that love with others.

Relationship is so vital in God's eyes that He gave us the capacity to carry out His purpose for our lives. In our roots back in the garden of Eden, there was a quality of life, an expression of true relationship so fulfilling we find ourselves longing for it today. Chuck Swindoll aptly describes the situation:

> *Nothing but innocence was flowing through the bloodstream of mankind. There was enviable, uninterrupted communion with the living God, mankind's Creator. There was the blessing and delight of walks with God, the joy of His presence, the unguarded relationship, the familiar friendship. There was an absence of rebellion, selfishness, defensiveness, and embarrassment.*[8]

Here is a profound, yet almost forgotten truth. At one time in human history we were perfectly capable of relating to God and one another—openly, honestly, without fear. This, in essence, is what we were created for. This is why we are.

Question 2: Where Are We?

The Bible clearly teaches that the human race got off to a remarkably promising start. In the beginning we were granted an environment, a nature, and a capacity for true and lasting goodness. But where have we gone from there? When we examine ourselves as a species, what do we see?

A Look Back

If we are truly interested in getting an accurate feel for our character as a species, a good place to begin is in the annals of history. Unfortunately, when we look to the record of our past, an unflattering picture begins to emerge.

In a stunning summary, the *Canadian Army Journal* estimates that since 3,600 B.C. there have been 14,531 wars resulting in the deaths of nearly 3.6 billion people. The monetary value of the destruction from these conflicts is great enough to pay for a gold belt 97.2 miles wide and 33 feet thick to stretch around the world. The study concludes that since 3,600 B.C. there have been only 292 years of peace. The Associated Press adds that the year 1986 set a new record for most wars on the planet at 22. The death toll from these conflicts alone is 2.2 million, with civilian casualties accounting for 84 percent of those killed. Is it any wonder that peace has been defined as the time it takes the nations to reload?

That Was Then, This Is Now

At this point some will argue, "Sure, humanity has a bad track record. But that is only the result of our primitive beginnings. We're evolving all the time. We're learning our lessons and getting better. Besides, wars are fought by nations. The individual people are basically good."

Does this popular line of thinking hold water? Consider an action by an individual as contemporary as today's headlines.

On Monday, December 7th, 1987, a Pacific Southwest Airlines jetliner rolled down the runway and lifted off into the hazy skies above Los Angeles. Its forty–three passengers and crew members were making a routine, even boring commuter hop up the coast to San Francisco.

The flight would never arrive.

On this trip, one of the passengers was a PSA supervisor named Raymond Thomson. It had not been an easy day on the job for Thomson. Earlier in the afternoon he had endured a less than friendly meeting with a fired employee named David Burke. Burke had been dismissed in November after a hidden camera filmed him allegedly stealing less than one hundred dollars from flight cocktail sales.

Unknown to Thomson, Burke had followed him onto the San Francisco flight. Somewhere over the central California coast, Burke scrawled an ominous message on the back of an airsick bag. "Hi Ray, I think it's sort of ironic that we end up like this. I asked for some leniency for my family, remember. Well, I got none and you'll get none."

Burke had managed to smuggle a .44 caliber Magnum Smith and Wesson handgun with him on the plane. According to CBS News, the cockpit conversation recording contained the voice of a flight attendant saying, "We've got a problem here." Another voice then responded, "I'm the problem."

The pilot reported shots fired, then the radio went dead. The plane's wreckage was found on an isolated hillside. The bitterness of one man cost forty–two lives.

Sharpening the Focus

When we examine the acts of nations and the acts of individuals, we are forced to take a hard look at ourselves. James Russell Lowell once remarked, "Whatever you may be sure of, be sure of this, that you are dreadfully like other people."

At this point, things get a little bit touchy. Our natural response is to distance ourselves from the murderer, the warmonger, the drug dealer, the wicked and perverse. But another recent news item demonstrated with uncomfortable clarity the fine line that separates the convicted criminal from the concerned citizen.

At 7:14 A.M. January 24, 1989, a pale, quiet, and submissive man was escorted into a stark, sparsely furnished room in the Florida State Prison in Gainesville. Strong hands forcefully guided him to his seat, but he offered little resistance. His resting place was a heavy oak chair, called "Old Sparky" by the inmates. His arms and legs were firmly secured, a leather strap was cinched under his chin, then a black veil was placed over his face. At 7:15 A.M. an anonymous executioner threw the switch. For a one minute cycle, two thousand volts at twelve amperes jolted through this man's body. At 7:16 A.M. a Gainesville coroner certified that Ted Bundy—a man called one of the most diabolically clever serial killers in history—was dead.

With over twenty mutilation and torture–style murders to his credit, few would point to Bundy as an example of the inherent goodness of man. But the presence of true, palpable evil wasn't snuffed out in the electric chair that cool Florida morning. According to a report filed by *Knight–Ridder* Newspapers, evil was doing land office business just outside the prison walls.

> *In the dark hours before dawn yesterday, a macabre carnival roared in a pasture across the street from the prison. Wearing costumes, waving signs, laughing and chattering, hundreds celebrated the impending execution. Some bundled up their toddlers and brought them along.*
>
> *An unidentified man came sporting his rubber Ronald Reagan mask and his "Burn Bundy" T-shirt. He dangled a child's stuffed bunny from a miniature noose.*
>
> *A chorus of middle-aged revelers waved sparklers and sang "On Top of Old Sparky" to the tune of "Old Smokey." "He bludgeoned the pooooor girls, all over the heeaad. Now we're all ecstatic, Ted Bundy is dead."*

> *Entrepreneurs capitalized on the gathering. A Starke restaurant—the owner wouldn't say which one—sold donuts and coffee. A man who gave his name only as Rick, from "central Florida" was selling tiny electric chair lapel pins at $5 a piece.*
>
> *The spectacle flickered and flared under the shifting gaze of TV floodlights and the air was poisonous with the exhaust from 10 acres of cars, recreational vehicles, and mobile broadcast units.[9]*

A Gainesville radio station went so far as to urge listeners to "give their appliances the morning off" so that Ted could get his full share of "juice." Who was less pleasing to God that terrible morning? The man who committed horrible atrocities and died in the chair, or the "upstanding, law–abiding citizens" who turned the bitter end of a long and incredibly painful ordeal into "fun for all ages"?

James Sewell, chief of the Gulfport, Florida Police Department, had taken part in the investigation of Bundy's attack and murder of two sorority sisters at Florida State University. Before entering the prison complex to witness the execution, he gazed at the carnival taking place across the street. "The victims of Ted Bundy deserve more than that. Theatrics don't belong here. It cheapens the whole process."

Wickedness, it seems, is a many–splendored thing.

With the sobriety of a cancer specialist delivering the bad news, the Bible states the sad facts of human existence. "There is none righteous, not even one; there is none who understands, there is none who seeks for God; all have turned aside, together they have become useless; there is none who does good, there is not even one" (Rom. 3:10–12).

Our pride rails against such a seemingly harsh verdict. Yet the truthfulness of this assessment haunts us. Even children, the most obvious symbol of innocence and purity, give us away. Consider the findings of the Minnesota Crime Commission on the essence of human nature found in children:

> *Every baby starts life as a little savage. He is completely selfish and self-centered. He wants what he wants when he wants it—his bottle, his mother's attention, his playmate's toy, his uncle's watch. Deny him these once, and he seethes with rage and aggressiveness, which would be murderous were he not so helpless. He is, in fact, dirty. He has no morals, no knowledge, no skills. This means that all children—not just certain children—are born delinquent. If permitted to continue in the self-centered world of his infancy, given free reign to his impulsive actions to satisfy his wants, every child would grow up a criminal—a thief, a killer, or a rapist.*[10]

The hard truth we must face is that whatever is possible for others is possible for us. Despite our wonderful environment and our amazing personal potential, we have willfully gone our own way.

The Heart of the Matter

The core issue that humanity must face is our use of free choice. Rather than creating a race of robots, God gave us the ability to accept or reject a love relationship with Him. The consequence of our misused freedom is devastating. We have alienated ourselves from the God who loves us.

Francis Schaeffer observed, "Man is lost because he is separated from God, his true reference point, by true moral guilt. But he will never be nothing. Therein lies the horror of his lostness. For man to be lost, in all his uniqueness and wonder, is tragic."

We have taken the priceless gift of free will and used it wrongly. Contemporary Christian singer Randy Stonehill expressed our situation aptly:

We are all foolish puppets
Who, desiring to be kings
Now lie pitiful and crippled
After cutting our own strings.

The evidence is in, the conclusion strikingly clear: All have sinned and fall short of the glory of God.

Question 3: Where Can We Be?

Some people look at our world, filled with inhumanity and evil, and declare that God is dead. Ironically, the Bible tells us that God looks at this same world, sees the same sad state of affairs, and declares that man is dead. Dead in the sense that without God's help we are incapable of truly relating to Him or to others.

Our condition is becoming more critical with each passing day. The destructive capabilities of nuclear weapons will soon be in the hands of a widening circle of stable and unstable world leaders. The global population continues to grow, especially in the Third World, where resources are becoming increasingly scarce. Unforeseen natural disasters seem only to intensify the pressure on an already beleaguered humanity.

The Truth Behind the Headlines

The British writer G. K. Chesterton once stated, "Countless acts by millions of self–centered, instead of God–centered, individuals may reasonably be thought to be destroying the world."

The hard truth is that our global crisis is nothing more than the aggregation of our individual crises. We watch the evening news, shake our heads and ask, *What's wrong with this world?* Then we get up out of our La–z–Boy recliner just long enough to get into a fight with our neighbor whose dog scattered garbage all over our front lawn. What is wrong with the world? The simple answer is that we, you and I as individuals, are the problem. The comic page philosopher Pogo once remarked, "We have met the enemy, and he is us." Pogo and G. K. Chesterton hit the nail on the head. The source of our human crisis isn't to be found in Washington or Moscow or Tehran. Our problem is rebellion against our Creator, a rebellion that resides in every human heart. *We* are what's wrong with this world.

A Glimmer of Hope

Is there an answer to our human dilemma?

The Bible says yes.

Understanding our true nature as people is the key to hope. If the source of our problems lies with the individual, so does the solution. Our world lies on the brink of disaster because we as people have turned our backs on the God who made us. Our only hope is to turn back to Him—one life at a time.

In 2 Corinthians (5:20–21), the apostle Paul made an impassioned appeal that is every bit as relevant today as the day it was penned over nineteen hundred years ago. "Therefore, we are ambassadors for Christ, as though God were entreating through us; we beg you on behalf of Christ, be reconciled to God. He made Him who knew no sin (Jesus) to be sin on our behalf, that we might become the righteousness of God in Him."

We live on a planet suffering the effects of alienation. The fact is we are separated from God. As we read headlines about humanity's almost unimaginable capacity for cruelty, violence, and selfishness, as we feel the deep ache of fractured and hurting relationships within our hearts, as we wrestle with our own conscience, despairing of ever finding a sense of meaning and purpose in life, we experience the consequences of this separation on a daily basis. But God, in His infinite love, offers us a way back to Him.

This opening of the ultimate road home was no small feat. As we have seen, humanity can be described in many ways, but innocent is not one of them. A God of pure goodness certainly couldn't welcome us into heaven without either being blind or unjust. The Bible tells us that God is the ultimate judge who will examine every detail of our lives with perfect integrity. He has no special favorites. He will never wink at our wrong–doing or look the other way. Justice demands that a verdict be reached and a price must be paid.

But the amazing truth is that God continues to love us in spite of our wrongs. He sent His only son, Jesus, to suffer and die in our place.

Many have a hard time understanding how the death of Jesus nearly two thousand years ago could pay the penalty for our moral failures. The account of an unusual trial "down under" can provide some insight.

> *Two close friends graduated from college in Australia. One became a judge and the other a banker. One day the banker was arrested for embezzlement of one million dollars. He was to be tried before his friend. There was great speculation in the press. Would the judge throw the book at his buddy, proving what a just judge he was? Or would he let his friend off free? The courtroom was packed. The jury deliberated. They delivered the verdict— guilty. The judge gave the sentence. He leveled the harshest fine possible against his friend. The crowd gasped in amazement. But then everyone watched in wonder as the judge stood, took off his robe, walked around the bar and extended his hand to his friend. He said, "I have sold my house, taken all my savings out of my account. I have paid the fine I just leveled against you." The judge was just and the judge was loving. Justice was honored. But friendship was honored too. And all in the one act of paying the fine. That is how it works with Christ's death on the cross. In one act both justice and love are found.*[11]

God has found a way to give us right standing before Him; a way completely independent of our I'll–do–better–

next–time attempts to live up to the Ten Commandments
or even the dictates of our own consciences. As one
commentator observed:

> *It is this sacrifice of Jesus that makes
> Christianity such a different religion. Other
> religions list lots of acts or states of mind that
> have to be achieved before God will accept a
> person. But this message from God says: "Yes,
> you are guilty. You have failed, sinned, ruined
> the perfect world. You can't be good enough.
> But I love you. I love you so much my own Son
> came to your planet and shared your sorrows.
> He took your punishment."[12]*

The first step to experiencing this powerful
reconciliation is to wake up and smell the coffee. We must
come to grips with our individual need. If we continue to
comfort ourselves with the notion that we are basically
good, we will never truly return to God. There is only one
way back—acknowledging our desperate need for the
forgiveness only God can give. We will only seek
forgiveness when we realize that we are the ones in the
wrong.

The Paradox of Humanity

We are many things as people. We have the ability to
love and to hate, to win and to lose, to help and to hurt.
But most of all, we have been given the power to choose.
God has given us the dignity of choice, a free choice, to
accept or reject a relationship with Him. Our choice will
have real consequences. We can spend our lives walking
with God or running from Him. We can invest our short
time here blaming God or being healed by Him. We can
deny Him, devote our lives to Him, or dimly acknowledge
His existence.

But whatever we decide to do, we must live with our
choice. What will you decide?

Discussion Questions

1. Read Luke 23:39–43. Do you believe the thief on the cross deserved to be with Jesus in paradise? Why or why not?

2. Do you find it easier to be open and honest about your faults or to keep them hidden away? Explain your answer.

3. Do you honestly believe that you are as much to blame for the sad state of this world as a criminal or a cruel dictator?

Why or why not?

4. Do you find it easier to forgive others, or to ask forgiveness for yourself? Does that tendency effect your relationship with God? In what ways?

Chapter V
To Thine Own
Self Be True

*To navigate by a landmark tied to your own
ship's head is ultimately impossible.*
— Paul Ramsey —

WEDNESDAYS WERE always a drag. From my eight–year–old point of view this, of all days of the week, was the lowlight. Nothing good was on TV. The teacher always gave out three hundred pages of homework in spelling or (horror of horrors!) math (fractions, no less!). Mom would serve something healthy with lots of vegetables. The world championship of driveway basketball never came together because Peter Huested had to get his hair cut. It was two whole days from the freedom of Saturday, but it felt like two years. Quiet, hopeless despair reigned on Wednesdays.

Then, around seven, my dad would make his way up the walk. As I sat in my room, swearing that I would plot my career in any line of work that didn't require adding 3/18ths and 11/3rds, he would open the door to share the only news that could lift such serious depression. "We've got the Dodger tickets for Saturday!"

I loved going to Dodger games. Even now just seeing a "Game of the Week" on Saturday morning can cause a flood of memories to come roaring back. The sight of the stadium as we came over the hill in the station wagon. Arguing with my big brother over whose favorite baseball player was the greatest. The smell of Dodger Dogs with lots of mustard and those breath-killing chopped white onions. The sound of the bat as a solid line drive headed for left field. From my eight–year–old vantage it didn't get any better than this.

As I sat in the stands, first baseman's mit ready for a foul ball (I just knew one would head our way), it began to hit me. Wes Parker, Jim Lefebvre, and the rest of the Dodgers had it made. Not only did they get to play baseball every day (and undoubtedly never had to worry about fractions), they got paid for it as well! I, on the other hand, stood around in left field for the Somis Saints for free. In fact, I even had to work one Saturday at the dreaded Somis Little League annual pancake breakfast for the privilege. As I sat in the second deck of Dodger Stadium, spilling my soft drink on the people in front of me, I made up my mind. When I grew up, I wanted to get paid to do something I loved.

Lo and behold, I have been able to realize that ambition. I now make my living talking with people about the greatest source of satisfaction and joy in my life, a personal relationship with God. This line of work certainly isn't all sunshine and flowers, but it is never boring. And if you keep your eyes and ears open, it's possible to gain some fascinating insights into human nature and culture.

Recently I had the opportunity to discuss spiritual perspectives with a highly successful professional man. He had earned advanced degrees from a top university and was extremely articulate and thoughtful. Our conversation focused on the person of Jesus Christ, the possibility of miracles, and ultimately the meaning of life. Fairly heavy stuff to be kicking around on a late Sunday afternoon.

As we talked, it became apparent that we represented two very different points of view. To draw our discussion to an end on a positive note, he offered a summary statement that he was sure we could both agree upon: "Well, Scott, it's like the Good Book says, 'To thine own self be true.'"

After a moment of awkward silence, I replied, "I don't mean to sound like a smart aleck, but the Bible never teaches that point of view. That quote is from Shakespeare; Hamlet, as I recall." (I didn't have the heart to mention that the character who uttered those immortal words was the buffoon of the play.)

After a few minutes of hemming and hawing and "you–know–what–I–means," our conversation drew to an end, but the impact has remained for me. The interaction I was able to have with this man was a real eye–opener, and it revealed two key facts about the religious climate of our day. First, even highly educated and intelligent people are woefully uninformed about the message of the Bible. Second, the average person isn't concerned about spiritual facts because we're convinced that truth, particularly spiritual truth, is in the eye of the beholder. Truth is strictly lower case. Spiritual reality, we're told, is completely relative with no basis in fact.

The Relative Thinking Influence Test

To grasp how firmly entrenched this perspective has become, take this brief subjective thinking influence test. Imagine yourself at a major university. You walk into a huge lecture hall filled with sharp–looking students. An intimidatingly academic–looking professor, replete with pipe and a tweed jacket with elbow patches, saunters to the front of the class. He welcomes you to Philosophy 101 and announces that your first exercise is to briefly state your basic understanding of life and ultimate reality. Which of these statements would you feel more comfortable making before the class?

A. "I believe in absolute truth. There are standards of right and wrong that apply to every person, in every situation."

B. "I believe that truth is a personal thing, and if something is true for you, then go with it. But don't push your morality on others."

The choice in this philosophy class is clear. If we want to avoid conflict, a round of boos and hisses, or being perceived as a fanatic from the dim recesses of the Puritan past, we'll choose "B." If we wish to enjoy a long, hard, uphill fight of a semester, with lots of delightful red marks all over our papers, we'll take a deep breath and go for "A."

We live in a society that has bought heavily into a subjective view of truth. Fritz Perls's statement, "You go your way, I'll go mine, if we meet in the middle it's beautiful" could replace "In God We Trust" on our currency. But there are some serious questions that advocates of subjective truth must answer. Are there really no absolutes? If it "works for you" does that make it right? Is it possible to be "true to ourselves" and false toward God and others?

The Risk of Relative Thinking

On the pages of Charles Schultz's comic strip "Peanuts," the junior pop philosopher Linus came face to face with a form of religious persecution. In an understandable piece of children's logic, he decided that Halloween was just as important an occasion as Christmas. If Christmas had Santa Claus, why shouldn't Halloween have a hero as well? So Linus used his imagination and invented a suitable mythical figure for the occasion—the Great Pumpkin. Naturally, this departure from the straight and narrow met with some opposition. Linus ended up being ridiculed by the holders of the more traditional belief in Santa and the eight tiny reindeer. But, undaunted, security blanket in hand, he uttered a phrase that would become an anthem for a generation: "It doesn't matter what you believe, as long as you're sincere!"

Linus had put into words the feelings of many. Tolerance of any and every spiritual point of view is highly admired in our culture. To critically evaluate the content of a belief system has come to be seen as a social *faux pas* in the same category as slurping your soup or belching at the dinner table.

The popularity of a subjective perspective on truth isn't difficult to understand. It has the same appeal as youth soccer or the Special Olympics. No matter what your belief, everyone wins. All roads lead to heavenly rewards. I will be seen by others as open–minded and good–hearted if I remain noncommittal about truth.

It also sounds safe. If there is no ultimate right or wrong, I won't have to worry about explaining the dark side of my life to God, who may not buy my clever rationale for living to satisfy my primal urges.

Furthermore, it has the feel of the moral high ground. The ultimate sin (at least the one that gets you on the cover of the *National Enquirer*) is hypocrisy. If being a hypocrite is the failure to live up to the standards of your belief, the safest way to avoid hypocrisy is simple; eliminate the standards one might have trouble keeping. You know, those obnoxious ones like "Thou shalt not covet" or "Thou shalt not commit adultery"—the ones that require moral discipline. With a little editing, the Ten Commandments aren't so bad after all, and we can commend ourselves as being morally upright for doing what we would have done anyway.

In an interview on "The Today Show," actress Liv Ullman captured the essence of this school of modern ethics. "There are no rules which apply to everybody and there are many kinds of truths. The one which is easiest and best to live by is your own, the core within yourself. I've never told my daughter that what I say is the truth." The message is abundantly clear. True or false have been rendered irrelevant. Just believe and do what is "easiest and best" for you.

This sort of thinking sounds great on "Entertainment Tonight" or in the hallowed halls of higher learning, but can we consistently live with the philosophy that truth is elastic and sincerity is all that counts in the real world of day–to–day life?

A Nightmare on Glebe Street

Consider the adventures of a very sincere wrecking crew in Australia. Journalist David Osborne was excited about the purchase of his new home at 58 Glebe Street in the suburbs of Sydney. Renovations were nearly complete, and he was due to move in within a week. After work, he drove to his new address to check on some of the final details. When Osborne arrived that fateful Monday afternoon, he found a "what's–wrong–with–this–picture" scenario beyond his ability to believe. His dream home had become a nightmare. A huge crane with a wrecking ball towered over his property. Every floor in the house had been removed. Thousands of dollars in renovation materials including a valuable antique fireplace had been transformed into a large pile of debris. Standing in the rubble that was his home was New South Wales Housing Minister Frank Walder who offered this explanation: "The contractor and demolition crew were told to go to 58 Glebe *Point Road*, but instead went to 58 Glebe *Street*." Oops! Sorry about that.

How would you react if you were in Osborne's shoes? Here was a completely sincere wrecking crew. They were so sincere in their belief that they had the right address, they demolished your beautiful new home. Could you imagine saying, "Well, it doesn't really matter, as long as you worked very hard and sincerely while destroying my house"? In day–to–day life we demand precision. Sincere, subjective thinking doesn't prevent large lawsuits.

The Hindu and the Tea Kettle

Subjective thinking runs into difficulties in the realm of personal belief as well. Susan Schaeffer Macaulay in her provocative book, *How to Be Your Own Selfish Pig*, shares an insightful cross–cultural encounter.

> One afternoon, my parents visited Cambridge University and met with some students in the living room of a college apartment. My husband-to-be, Ranald, his good friend Tom, and other students gathered around the fireplace. A tea kettle was whistling cheerfully on a gas burner nearby promising hot cups of tea.
>
> As the group discussed ideas, one young man from India, who was Hindu by religion, started to speak out against Christian ideas of truth. My father decided to probe this fellow's own conclusions, to show that he could not actually live and act upon what he said he believed.
>
> "Are we agreed," my father asked, "that you believe there is only one reality, which includes all things, all ideas?"
>
> The young man nodded.
>
> "Then," my father pursued, "this means that ultimately everything is the same. Any difference we see is temporary, an illusion. There is no such thing as a separate personality, correct? No final difference between good and evil, or between cruelty and non-cruelty?" The young man agreed again, but the others in the room were surprised at what the full extent of their friend's Hindu beliefs could be.
>
> Tom was struck with the fact that such beliefs didn't fit into the real world. But instead of arguing, he reached for the steaming tea kettle, lifted it off the gas burner, and held it over the startled Indian's head. Everyone looked surprised, and the Indian student looked scared to death.
>
> "If what you believe is really true," Tom said firmly, "there is no ultimate difference between cruelty and non-cruelty. So whether I choose to pour this boiling water over your head or not doesn't matter."

> *There was a moment of silence, and then the Indian rose and left the room without comment. He could not match what he believed with real life.*[13]

Truth can be a dangerous thing. It is quite patient and relentless. And it is unaffected by majority vote, Gallup Polls, or the latest consensus of the scientific community. As columnist William Pfaff observes:

> *This year and last year... we are all anti-racist. Why are we anti-racist? We know that it is right. How do we know? Fifty years ago black people certainly knew it, but it seems fair to say that at that time most white people, in or out of Western civilization, took for granted a natural inferiority of black people. A hundred years ago science and the universities offered serious theories justifying racial hierarchy and racist public policies. Seventy-five years ago most Gentile Europeans and North Americans were probably to some degree, often virulently so, anti-Semitic. Fifty years ago the most powerful political movement in Europe attempted to exterminate the Jewish people, holding that this was not only the "right" thing to do but was scientifically justified. In both cases, minorities resisted the majority on the grounds of a value system that insisted on the absolute worth of the individual person, and in the belief that truth has nothing to do with the prevailing power system. Eventually they won.*
>
> *Who can say what people may believe or do 50 or 100 years from now... if nothing is objectively true, values and moral reasoning are merely power games. If they are power games, truth is defined by power—and the only moral difference between you and Hitler is that he lost a war.*[14]

The impact of our view of truth is staggering because the power of truth, absolute truth, is staggering. No matter how eloquent our protests, no matter how well worked out our rationale for denying its existence, sooner or later truth affects us all.

Go Play on the Freeway

My first day in a college philosophy class drove this point home. Our professor was fairly young to be in his position and seemed a little nervous about his "live" debut. His first glance at the class was so furtive and tension–filled it made me think of the look of sheer terror I'd seen before only in the eyes of a "B" grade horror movie victim (immediately before being swallowed by a mutant carrot from outer space) or a junior high substitute teacher (immediately before being swallowed by a mutant pack of seventh graders). To compensate for his case of the jitters, he decided to go on the offensive. "Welcome to Philosophy 101. Let me promise you, this won't be just another boring class. Our goal is to challenge and evaluate our way of thinking, even about those ideas you take for granted. Our first assignment will be to read and discuss Berkeley's classic work, *Three Dialogues Between Hylas and Philonous.* In this study, Berkeley proved that matter doesn't exist." Much to the chagrin of our fledgling Socrates, a football player in the class (who had considerable personal experience with matter in large quantities) laughed at the idea. The professor challenged him to a duel of wits, and began to reel off Berkeley's chain of reasoning. Some twenty minutes and a full chalk board later, the professor turned confidently to the football player and triumphantly said, "So we can see, matter doesn't exist. Any questions?"

"Yeah. If you're so sure matter doesn't exist, why don't you go play on the freeway and prove it?"

The Fork in the Road

What the nature of day–to–day life indicates, the Bible makes explicit. There exists a reality that is unaffected by human opinion, no matter how sincere. Contrary to what celebrity philosophers like Liv Ullman or Shirley MacLaine may teach, absolute truth, binding on all people, is a fact of life. And according to Jesus, speaking in His Sermon on the Mount, how we deal with the truth can decide our destiny after death.

Christians are often chided in secular circles for making statements like, "There's only one way, one truth, and one life." Would it surprise you to learn that in the Sermon on the Mount Jesus speaks of two ways, two truths, and two lives?

Two Ways

"Enter by the narrow gate; for the gate is wide, and the way is broad that leads to destruction, and many are those who enter by it. For the gate is small, and the way is narrow that leads to life, and few are those who find it" (Matt. 7:13–14).

Could you imagine the uproar a statement like this would cause on the Phil Donahue Show? Consider the implications of this two–sentence bombshell. According to no less an authority than Jesus Christ, everyone is not headed for heaven. The sad fact is the vast majority are moving in the opposite direction, and sincerity does precious little to alter their final destination. The good news is that people continue to live beyond the grave. The sobering news is that there are only two ways leading to our final destination: One leads to destruction; one leads to life.

Two Truths

Jesus continued,

> *Beware of the false prophets, who come to you in sheep's clothing, but inwardly are ravenous wolves. You will know them by their fruits. Grapes are not gathered from thorn bushes, nor figs from thistles, are they? Even so, every good tree bears good fruit; but the bad tree bears bad fruit. A good tree cannot produce bad fruit, nor can a bad tree produce good fruit. Every tree that does not bear good fruit is cut down and thrown into the fire. So then, you will know them by their fruits* (Matt. 7:15–20).

In this passage, Jesus issues a warning to His listeners. In essence He gives humanity a spiritual wake–up call. Christ says that the hard fact is not every religious teacher is good. Not every prophet speaks for God. Not every religious system vying for our attention is true.

Consider the career of a prominent Northern California pastor. The emphasis of his "ministry" was to reach those that the traditional church turned away. He accomplished so much practical good for the poor that his work was recognized by leading political figures of his day. He was a magnetic orator and his fledgling church mushroomed. He was guided by a vision of founding a utopian community where his followers could apply his teachings without interference or harassment. This "city on a hill" became a reality. Named in honor of Reverend Jim Jones, Jonestown sprung up on the map of Guyana almost overnight. Tragically, the fruit of Jim Jones's ministry was forthcoming. He began to believe that he was an incarnation of Jesus Christ. His followers began to believe it as well. When the U.S. government began to investigate charges of forced labor in Jonestown, this false prophet did the unthinkable. The more than eight hundred sincere men, women and children who followed Jones to South America perished in a macabre communal service that featured cyanide–laced punch.

Or consider the impact of a European political reformer. Before he came to power it took over one trillion of his government's bills to equal one dollar. But after a few years under his leadership, a broken and bankrupt nation rose to world prominence. Such ability rarely goes unnoticed. This leader won the admiration of many of the intellectual elite of his day. The French academician Louis Bertrand described him by saying, "What sovereign, what national hero has ever been acclaimed, adulated, adored and worshipped as has this little man in the brown shirt... This is something altogether different from mere popularity, this is *religion*. In the eyes of his admirers Hitler is a prophet, the partaker of the divine." The teaching of this "prophet" led to nearly fifty million deaths as it found its fruition in World War II.

Jesus said that we would hear the words of both true and false prophets, and that the validity of their spiritual teaching was never to be determined by sincerity alone. Few have been more sincere about their beliefs than Adolph Hitler or Jim Jones. Few have demonstrated their sincerity more concretely than the followers of these men, literally dying for their faith in the bitter cold of the Russian front or in the steamy jungle of Jonestown.

Christ's message is simple. We can place our faith in one of two versions of the truth. The truth according to man or the truth according to God.

Two Lives

Jesus continued, "Not everyone who says to Me, 'Lord, Lord,' will enter the kingdom of heaven; but he who does the will of My Father who is in heaven. Many will say to Me on that day, 'Lord, Lord, did we not prophesy in Your name, and in Your name cast out demons, and in Your name perform many miracles?' And then I will declare to them, 'I never knew you; depart from me, you who practice lawlessness'" (Matt. 7:21–23).

Insurance agents, TV weatherforecasters, and tea leaf readers have managed to enjoy a good livelihood over the years trading on a common, practical desire of almost all of humanity: people want to anticipate and plan for the future. In this passage, Jesus gives us the ultimate, practical look–ahead.

There will be only two kinds of life awaiting us after death. One form of eternal life will be spent enjoying the presence of God. The other will be spent excluded from Him.

Heaven or Hell?

For a number of years there was a consensus in our culture that when all was said and done here on earth, heaven was definitely the place we wanted to be. These days some people are not so sure. After all, if heaven is simply floating along on a cloud, plucking on a harp while wearing a decidedly unstylish robe, or (even worse) something like a cosmic church service that lasts forever (with no hope of running home to catch the Rams game afterward), what's the big attraction, anyway?

On the other hand, some are amending hell to be, well, not so bad after all. They envision it as being maybe a little bit like the Las Vegas Strip during mid–July, but without air conditioning. Some have even been so bold as to declare, "Hell will be great. I'm looking forward to it. All my buddies will be there. We'll play some poker and party forever!"

What will heaven and hell be like in reality? A crucial biblical insight into ultimate reality is expressed concisely in the book of James: "Every good thing bestowed and every perfect gift is from above, coming down from the Father of lights, with whom there is no variation, or shifting shadow" (James 1:17).

It has been said that earth is as close as a person who rejects God will ever get to heaven, and as close as a person who knows God will ever get to hell. The Bible tells us that all the good things we experience in this life are a gift from God. In fact they are a reflection of His personality and nature. God's gifts come in all shapes and sizes: The comforting warmth of friendship grown soft, yet sturdy over time; the sense of peace we feel after a job well done; that sweet extra five minutes of sleep after the alarm goes off on a cold winter morning; being able to shed a tear at a soft drink commercial (the one where a child hands a single rose to an armed–to–the–teeth border guard who smiles and sheepishly puts it in his lapel); the bemused sense of disbelief and pride we feel when our all–too–

quickly–grown–up child turns to us and says, "Mom and Dad, I love you."

These everyday blessings, so easily taken for granted, are the rough equivalent of an I–love–you note from the Almighty. But even more, these highlights of life are just previews of coming attractions. They are only the slightest foretaste of a forever with the One who built into us an overwhelming need for security, an overwhelming need to matter. Here on earth we hunger for love, pure, unconditional, and permanent. After a few bouts with broken relationships, unfulfilled expectations, or the bitter taste of loss, we wonder if the fulfilling love we're looking for could ever really exist. The marvelous news is that real love isn't some romantic pipe dream. In heaven we will know that love perfectly. The ache and frustration of our Don Quixote–like quest for personal peace on earth will be only a dim and fading memory. The fulfillment of all we were ever meant to be is what heaven is all about.

Hell, on the other hand, is anything but a party. The Bible describes it as an all too real place of isolation, frustration, and pain. Imagine a world with no love, no significance, no hope. Imagine a world without redeeming qualities, where despair is the order of never–ending days, where love is only a dim and fading memory, and we catch only the faintest glimpse of hell. No buddies, no good times, no bright lights. Only darkness, and being alone, living forever with ourselves and the thought of what might have been. *That* is hell.

In heaven, all the good will be refined, purified, and made right again. In hell, all the good will be gone. In this life we can experience the slightest taste of both final destinations. The odd mixture of pleasure and pain, grief, and joy we experience here on earth is as close as a person who rejects God will ever get to heaven, and as close as a person who knows God will ever get to hell.

A Crucial Question

What is the difference between those who will spend eternity with God and those who won't? It isn't a matter of words. Those who reject God will emphatically call after Christ "Lord! Lord!" It isn't a matter of religious acts. Those who reject God present a nice resume of spiritual activities to recommend themselves, including the seemingly miraculous. The watershed issue is doing "the will of my Father Who is in heaven," coming to God on His terms.

What does it mean to come to God on His terms? This question was hot on the minds of those who heard Jesus speak. "They said therefore to Him, 'What shall we do, that we may work the works of God?' Jesus answered and said to them, 'This is the work of God, that you believe in Him whom He has sent'" (John 6:28–29).

Few careers demand more attention to the fine points of human interaction than that of a diplomat. Those who work in the foreign service branch of government quickly realize that there are right ways and wrong ways to approach those in power. For the U. S. Ambassador to Great Britain to approach the Queen of England, slap her on the back, and say, "Hey Liz baby! How's it goin'?" would be a disaster of international proportions. Respect for the position and power of a dignitary requires that strict protocol be followed. This same respect for position is relevant to our relationship with God. Rather than approaching God in a self–styled manner, we must realize the full implications of Who we are dealing with. God has determined that a very specific protocol be followed by those who approach Him; a protocol called faith.

We are restored to a right relationship with God only by placing our trust in Christ's death and resurrection on our behalf Jesus made it possible for us to live forever with God in heaven. We can add nothing to what Christ has done for us. All we must do is trust God and take Him up on His offer of life.

Paul summed up God's terms this way: "If you confess
with your mouth Jesus as Lord, and believe in your heart
that God raised Him from the dead, you shall be saved"
(Rom. 10:9–10).

No other way, no matter how sincerely followed, no
matter how ardently believed, can bring us into a personal
relationship with God.

Go with the Flow?

This truth stands in stark contrast to the especially
popular current notion that all religions teach the same
thing and that all spiritual rivers flow to the one great
ocean, which is God. If this were true, we would expect to
find a great deal of harmony in the basic tenets of the
major world religions. But is that the case?

Eastern mysticism teaches that God is an all–
encompassing, impersonal oneness; Islam, Judaism, and
Christianity state that God is not only personal, He's quite
distinct from His creation. Some religions hold that God is
fierce and brutal and must be appeased by quaint little
rituals like human sacrifice; others maintain that God loves
mankind and that each human life is sacred and worth
fighting for. Some state that the only way to please God is
to participate rigorously in a "laundry list" of rituals and
religious acts; Christianity maintains that we cannot earn
heaven by good deeds. We are forgiven for our past and
given a chance to forever experience the joy of God's
presence solely on the basis of His mercy and unmerited
favor.

Even a cursory examination of world religions shows
that those maintaining that these diverse points of view
are leading in the same direction have some serious
explaining to do. To please God do we polish our
personality or try to obliterate it? Is God a person, a barn
yard animal, or a charismatic leader tooling by in a Rolls
Royce? All these views may be wrong, but they certainly

can't all be right. The truth claims of one clearly exclude the others.

We must choose, and our choice of religious outlook boils down to a question of confidence. We need to honestly ask ourselves which point of view is solid enough to trust with our eternal destiny.

This is no trivial decision. If we came down with a case of athlete's foot at the health club we might be content to ask the sweaty guy in the next locker what he uses to deal with it. But if we suspected that we were facing a life–threatening illness, such as cancer, we would demand to see a qualified specialist. Our spiritual well–being should require the same intense concern. In His sinless life, His clear teaching about God and the human condition, and His death and resurrection, Jesus Christ has presented compelling credentials that He is worthy of our trust.

Of Oil and Bullets

Truth matters. We can sincerely believe that human flight is possible by jumping out of a three–story window and flapping our arms, but our sincerity doesn't make the sidewalk any softer. Sincerity didn't lessen the potency of the cyanide punch in Jonestown. Sincerity didn't defuse the bombs that laid waste to Germany at the end of World War II. Sincerity is a worthless virtue unless it is invested in truth.

In Soroti, Uganda, they learned this lesson the hard way. In November, 1987, a large group of anti–government rebels had targeted a rural army post and airstrip for take over. A company numbering in the hundreds gathered in the dense surrounding brush for the attack. But this was to be no ordinary invasion. The task force would use some strikingly unconventional tactics.

According to the Associated Press, the rebels attacked half–naked. A few wore old army trousers, a few wore army boots, and all of them had their pants rolled up above their knees. Curiously, all of the attackers were smeared with oil. As they advanced on the airstrip, they marched boldly, even fearlessly toward the government defending forces. In unison they chanted, "God is there! God is there!"

When the hour–long attack was over, the rebels were routed. Out of seven hundred men, two hundred were killed, many more were taken prisoner. One of the prisoners, a man named Obone, explained the bizarre event. The rebels were members of a disgruntled religious/political group called the "Holy Spirit Movement." The founder of this movement, a witch doctor named Alice Lakwena, convinced her forces that she had concocted magic oil that would protect them from bullets. She instructed them to take off their shirts, roll up their pant legs, and smear their bodies with the oil. She promised that rocks would explode like hand grenades for the faithful. The rag tag militia then went to take the airstrip and wait for foreign assistance. The troops never took the airstrip, and the foreign assistance never came. The battle was lost before it had begun.

No one could fault the "Holy Spirit Movement" for a lack of sincerity. One must be a true believer to face live bullets half naked. Sincere? Yes. But wrong, dead wrong.

Real Truth? Absolutely!

In contrast to our subjective and self–styled perspectives, Christ offers the real truth. Truth that can be tested in the crucible of day–to–day reality. Truth that we can base our lives on. As one–time–atheist C. S. Lewis remarked, "I believe in Christianity as I believe the sun has risen, not only because I see it, but because by it I see everything else."

Truth is a key issue. And the truth Christ presents forces us to answer two critical questions.

The first is, what is our source of truth? Will we gamble our ultimate destiny on a gut level hunch or warm feeling?

Or will we ask, honestly, does absolute truth, binding on all people at all places and times, exist?

Many today struggle with the idea of absolute truth. Those who insist on seeing the world in a black or white perspective are usually chastised by those who have become comfortable with shades of gray. The only constant we know is change, so what is true today may not be true tomorrow. What is true for the upscale yuppie "doing lunch" in L.A. may not be true for the bushman of the Kalahari. Right?

Those who reject the notion of absolute truth strongly assert that truth is totally dependent on time and place. Some even take the argument a step further and maintain that truth is relative to the worldview of every individual. A Christian believes that Jesus is the son of God and that is true "for her." A follower of Islam denies that God has a son and that is true "for him." It all depends on personal belief.

Is this really the case? Or is it possible that truth may be less elastic than we've been led to believe? Is it possible that there are some things that are always true, everywhere, for everyone?

Truth Is No Picnic

Consider a day in the life of a happy owner of a BMW in Los Angeles. He leaves his "power lunch" only to step outside and discover the weather is not exactly chamber of commerce picture day material. He gets on his car phone, dials up his wife, and breaks the bad news: "Muffy? Skip here. No can do on the 'Brie–a–thon' picnic. It's raining poodles and persians today."

Our yuppie has done more than simply convey an accurate observation of the weather. He has made an absolutely true statement, a statement that is equally true for the bushman making his way through the parched South African desert. It doesn't matter that it hasn't rained in a hundred days in the Kalahari, it is still absolutely true that at the day and time the yuppie makes his observation it is raining in L.A. Perspective, geography, or the time on the clock may change the way we view reality, but reality remains unchanged. When reality is described accurately, we encounter truth. Absolute truth.

Up on the Rooftop, Reindeer Pause?

This same principle applies to far more than the weather; it also extends into the realm of personal belief. For many of us, our first encounter with a *bona fide* crisis of faith was probably in the second grade. For as long as we could remember, we looked forward to Christmas. Aside from the inconvenience of entertaining distant relatives whose television habits included watching sappy programs like "Nanny and the Professor," the holidays were a positive experience. After all, everyone knew that on Christmas Eve, Santa would leave his toy shop at the North Pole, hitch Rudolf and his friends to the sleigh, and reward children all over the world for cleaning up their act for a whopping two weeks in December. Our faith in the jolly old elf went uncontested until some bratty kid, wolfing down a sugar cookie at the annual second grade Christmas party, puffed up his chest and said, "There ain't no such thing as Santa. It's just a gag your mom and dad pull on ya every year!" Opinion was fairly evenly divided among second graders on this crucial issue, and impassioned speeches both pro and con that Saint Nick could be heard echoing across the playground at recess. Sincerity of belief and disbelief was in abundance.

Who was telling the truth? Many today would smile and diplomatically dodge the issue by saying, "Well, Santa is real for the child who believes in him."

And for the smart aleck blowing cookie crumbs on his neighbor? "Well, Santa isn't true for the child who doesn't believe."

Sentimentality and *A Miracle on 34th Street* aside, there is an absolute answer to our second grade semi–theological debate. That answer must correspond to reality. An Arctic explorer can tell us if the Claus family does have a bungalow at the North Pole. We could assemble a number of witnesses to tell us conclusively if that "E–Z to Assemble Deluxe Swing Set" was really put together by a group of industrious elves or by a bleary–eyed, caffeine–driven parent.

The fact that some second graders ardently believe in Santa and some do not has no effect on whether Santa exists in reality. The fact that Santa exists as a nice custom and not as the actual being he is portrayed as at Christmas is an absolute truth. Absolute truth, always true for everyone, everywhere, is a fact of life. We cannot brush off a serious consideration of spiritual issues by saying, "Oh, that's nice for you, but not for me."

Jesus forces us to take a long hard look at the issue of truth. He claimed that we could know the truth (John 8:32), that the truth was verifiable (John 14:10–11), and that He Himself was the embodiment of truth (John 14:6). He was and is always true, for everyone, everywhere.

Papa's Perspective

The second, and equally important question raised by Christ is who will I be true to? Do I live for my fleeting desires and passing urges, or is there more to life than dying with the most accomplishments, experiences, or possessions?

Few men have more fully embodied the "to thine own self be true" philosophy than Ernest Hemingway. Author, revolutionary, big game hunter, lover, there were few experiences "Papa" missed in his meteoric stint on planet Earth. Yet, as the years took their toll and his senses dulled, life lost its attraction. Near the end Hemingway wrote, "I live in a vacuum that is as lonely as a radio tube when the batteries are dead and there is no current to plug into." Hemingway discovered the hard, cold truth. The problem with living to be "true to yourself" is that you end up having to live *with* yourself. This was a burden too great to bear; "Papa" took his own life with a shotgun blast.

How we face truth is a monumental decision. It will affect our lives, our deaths, and our forever after. As C. S. Lewis wrote, "Look for yourself, and you will find in the long run only hatred, loneliness, despair, rage, ruin, and decay. But look for Christ and you will find Him, and with Him everything else thrown in."

A Killer Illustration

In my background in public speaking, I have learned to leave the audience with a "killer" illustration, something that I want people to remember even if they forget everything else I said. In my studies of great public speakers, I have found no one who compares with Jesus Christ in leaving an impression on an audience. I finish this chapter with His "killer" illustration, from His most famous public address, the Sermon on the Mount. Jesus left his listeners with this classic parable.

> *Therefore everyone who hears these words of Mine, and acts upon them, may be compared to a wise man, who built his house upon the rock. And the rain descended, and the floods came, and the winds blew, and burst against that house; and yet it did not fall, for it had been founded upon the rock. And everyone who hears these words of Mine, and does not act upon them, will be like a foolish man, who built his house upon the sand. And the rain descended, and the floods came, and the winds blew, and burst against that house; and it fell, and great was its fall* (Matt. 7:24–27).

Will we be true to ourselves, or true to Christ?

Where are you building your house?

Discussion Questions

1. Read Matthew 5:17–19. How would you describe Jesus' attitude toward the Bible? Would most people today agree or disagree with Him on this point? Explain your answer?

2. If given the choice between an absolute or relative view of truth, which would most people choose today? Why?

3. Have you ever sincerely believed something, only to discover you were sincerely wrong? What did you learn from the experience?

4. A friend shares the belief that all people should do what is easiest and best for them personally. How would you respond?

CHAPTER VI

GOD HELPS THOSE
WHO HELP THEMSELVES

*I have great faith in fools; self-confidence my
friends call it.*

— Edgar Allen Poe —

ONE OF the surest signs that we are getting along in life
is the inevitable middle age disease of becoming domestic.
Remember all those things you hated to do with your
parents during your "wonder years"? Yard work? Going to
the hardware store? I was convinced that life in a Soviet
labor camp had to be better than the excruciating,
unrelenting boredom of the mulch department of the local
"Green Thumb" nursery.

The years have a way of roaring by. One minute we're in
junior high, trying desperately to get our locker open. The
next we're in college, trying desperately to get Mom and
Dad to send a little extra cash for the month. But the
ultimate benchmark, the ultimate reminder that the hands
of time are ever on the move, is that frightening Saturday
morning when you catch yourself leaving the house saying,
"Honey! I'm heading to the 'Green Thumb' to pick up some
mulch!"

Slowly but surely, even the most impatient little kid
grows up and becomes domestic. Yard work and the
hardware store become part of our weekend routine, and

with the cost of professional repairs these days, sooner or later we end up vying for the coveted crown of "Mr. Do–It–Yourself America."

My first encounter with this venerable tradition began innocently enough one lazy, Saturday evening in spring. I was about the very domestic business of incinerating hamburgers on the backyard patio grill when a large bug landed on my shoulder. Since large bugs are an Arizona tradition, I flicked it off and went back to managing my growing barbeque inferno. But taking a second look, I noticed something peculiar. This was no garden variety desert bug; this was a potentially pain producing wasp. When I glanced overhead I discovered that this was no loner! He and a few of his buddies had constructed a wasp condo on my patio overhang, and they weren't too pleased with the first stage smog alert from my hamburger smoke.

The logical, sensible next step was to call the exterminator. But, being a self–respecting American, I believed that there was no problem that couldn't be solved by hard work and personal know–how. I decided to "do it myself."

I found a company that specialized in pest control for the rank amateur and told them my sad tale of insect invasion.

The clerk wore a pair of dirty overalls with a name tag that said, "Hi! I'm Gus."

"Hmm," Gus said, stroking his bristly chin. "Sounds to me like you need a can of this here 'Wasp–Freeze.'"

Since "Wasp-Freeze" sounded like a bizarre flavor of the month at an ice cream store, I asked, "Is this stuff any good?"

"Good?" Gus retorted, smirking at my ignorance. "Look at what it says on the can. 'Wasp Freeze' kills those critters by smothering, radically lowering their body temperature, and destroying their little central nervous systems!"

I wondered if the Pentagon had heard of this stuff. "So all I need to do is spray them with this and it's all over, right?"

"Yep. Just remember two things. Spray 'em at night. They're less active then. And if you don't get 'em all on the first shot, one might pull a suicide run at you. But don't worry, you'll win."

Gus had made a sale. I left the store fully equipped for combat, the proud owner of eight cans of "Wasp–Freeze."

That evening, I prepared for battle with the meticulous precision of a Green Beret. Over my clothes I put on a particularly ratty sweat shirt with a draw string hood. My wife suggested that the smell of my sweats alone would probably wipe out the entire nest. (Just like a woman to joke before a man goes into combat.) Ski gloves on my hands, goggles over my eyes, my lucky Cubs cap on top of my hooded head; I was all set. I checked the time; nice and late. Not only would the wasps be in dreamland, but the risk of one of my neighbors spotting me in my ridiculous get–up would be kept to a bare minimum.

Rambo–like, I lumbered out the back door, ready to accomplish my deadly mission.

Suddenly, a loud noise from the back fence cut through the still night air. My neighbor and his sons were laughing their heads off at my anti–wasp outfit.

"Hi Bill. Hi Tim. How's it going?" I mumbled. What were they doing out at ten at night anyway? Oh well, I had bigger things on my mind. This threat to life, liberty, and the pursuit of safe barbecuing had to be removed.

I spotted the nest. Four or five docile looking wasps were visible on the outside. With a Clint Eastwood–like sneer on my face, I carefully took aim, and slowly pressed the trigger.

Gus was right; it was a piece of cake. The wasps dropped helplessly and instantly to the patio concrete. Technology had triumphed over nature again. I took off my hood, cap, and goggles and laughed at victory. "Build a nest on my patio will ya? You obviously didn't know who you were dealing with!"

I laughed too soon. Something was seriously wrong. If all the wasps were dead, what was the loud buzzing noise I was hearing? I glanced at the nest and watched in terror as the only survivor, King Wasp, crawled out. More than a little irritated by this chemical assault, he took off and made a suicide run, stinger first, at my unprotected head. I ducked out of the way and in a blind panic began spraying "Wasp–Freeze" with the scientific precision of an angry skunk.

The results? One frozen King Wasp; one barbecue area that smelled like bug spray for a week; and one proud American. No matter how silly, inefficient, or incompetent it looked, I solved the problem. I did it myself!

Our culture thrives on self–sufficiency. How many times have we heard, "If you want a job done right, do it yourself"?

Perhaps it's our pioneer roots. Maybe it's our love affair with Horatio Alger stories, or even our cherished belief that any child can grow up to be president. We believe wholeheartedly that the best person is the independent person. The more self–sufficient, the more personally capable, the more autonomous, the better we are.

The strong value we place on self–reliance has become intrinsically woven into the fabric of our culture. This attitude has even become part and parcel of our spiritual thinking. Ben Franklin captured the essence of true American spirituality in *Poor Richard's Almanac* when he coined the popular motto, "God helps those who help themselves."

Is this true? Can we solve our spiritual problems by investing a little more elbow grease on our souls? Can we construct our own ladder to heaven "with a little help from the 'man upstairs'"? Can we find peace and tranquility by "getting our act together" on our own power, by our own initiative? Or is it possible that in order to find real peace and fulfillment in life, we need more than "a little help"? Could it be that we need a full–blown rescue operation?

The Question of a Generation

Since the late 1950s there have been few forces more influential on the thoughts, beliefs, and attitudes of our culture than popular music. Far from being mere entertainment or diversion, our taste in music has become so important it almost defines who we are. If you doubt this, observe the reaction of some average teenagers when you tell them their favorite band sounds like a pack of irate tom cats on a summer night.

Few have had greater influence on popular music (and the popular mind) than four formerly struggling musicians from Liverpool who carved their niche in history as the Beatles.

After dominating the music charts for more than a decade, the "fab four" went their separate ways, continuing to record on their own. One of the most popular songs to emerge from these solo efforts was John Lennon's haunting "Imagine":

> *Imagine there's no heaven...*
> *Imagine all the people*
> *Living for today.*

Lennon's words reflected the anxious questioning of the post '60's counter culture. Was God simply an antiquated relic of the stiff and staid "I Like Ike" generation, a dodge for those desperately afraid of true personal freedom? Could man find fulfillment in life without God simply by living for today?

The Old College Try

The twentieth century has given us a classic example of a brilliant man who strove consistently to do just that. His name was Bertrand Russell.

Born to aristocratic parents in late nineteenth century England, Russell demonstrated extraordinary intelligence from an early age. His passionate love for mathematics, philosophy, and linguistics quickly propelled him into prominence among the intellectual elite of his day. Although his views on pacifism and morality plunged him into scandal more than once, his awards and achievements were many, including the Nobel Prize for Literature in 1950. The Encyclopedia Britannica praises him as "one of the most widely varied and persistently influential intellects of the 20th century."

Russell had little use for Christianity, or any form of religion for that matter. In 1927 he published one of his most famous works, the scathing *Why I Am Not a Christian*. Later in life he was quoted as saying, "Christians hold that their faith does good, but other faiths do harm.... What I wish to maintain is that all faiths do harm." Here was a spiritually self–sufficient man. By Russell's way of thinking, God was less than nonessential; He was an annoyance. John Lennon wrote "Imagine" but Bertrand Russell lived it.

A life of achievement. A life of notoriety. A life of commitment to principle. Surely if ever anyone "did it himself," Bertrand Russell was that individual. He simply didn't need God. He found fulfillment and meaning completely on his own. Or did he?

In *Why I Am Not a Christian*, Russell clearly expressed his world view:

> *Man is the product of causes which had no pre-vision of the end they were achieving.... His origin, his growth, his hopes and fears, his loves and his beliefs are but the outcome of accidental collections of atoms.... No fire, no*

heroism, no intensity of thought and feeling, can preserve an individual life beyond the grave.... All the labor of all the ages, all the devotion, all the noonday brightness of human genius are destined to extinction in the vast death of the solar system, and the whole temple of man's achievement must inevitably be buried beneath the debris of a universe in ruins—all these things, if not quite beyond dispute, are yet so nearly certain that no philosophy that rejects them can hope to stand. Only within the scaffolding of these truths, only on the firm foundation of unyielding despair can the soul's habitation henceforth be safely built!

For all his accomplishments, for all his accolades, Bertrand Russell's brave new lifestyle didn't meet his aching spiritual need. In fact it left him in utter despair.

Imagine that.

Meanwhile, Back at the Temple

The time honored pursuit of personal fulfillment apart from a relationship with God isn't the sole domain of the atheist or agnostic. Those deeply concerned with religion can find themselves in the same leaking boat. Luke records a parable of Christ that shows that religious actions and a relationship with God can be two very different things.

And He also told this parable to certain ones who trusted in themselves that they were righteous, and viewed others with contempt: "Two men went into the temple to pray, one a Pharisee, and the other a tax-gatherer. The Pharisee stood and was praying thus to himself, 'God, I thank Thee that I am not like other people: swindlers, unjust, adulterers, or even like this tax-gatherer. I fast twice a week; I pay tithes of all that I get.' But the tax-gatherer, standing some distance away, was even unwilling to lift up his eyes to heaven, but was beating his breast, saying, 'God, be merciful to me, the sinner!' I tell you, this man went down to his house justified rather than the

> *other; for everyone who exalts himself shall be humbled, but he who humbles himself shall be exalted"* (Luke 18:9-14).

The sobering truth Jesus sets out in this parable stands in stark contrast to the "God helps those who help themselves" theology of Ben Franklin. The Pharisee, a leading religious figure of his time, saw himself as a real credit to God and as a great example for others. He didn't rip off others in business dealings, he strove for fairness in interpersonal relationships, and he maintained fidelity in his marriage. To top it off, he did all the nice religious things expected of him, parting with food and even his money for God. Yes sir, God was sure lucky to have such an outstanding model of conspicuous piety on His team. All these fine activities got our upstanding citizen one thing— a huge case of pride. This individual had fallen into the trap of self–generated, self–contained "devotion" that Jesus warned of in Matthew 6:5: "And when you pray, you are not to be as the hypocrites; for they love to stand and pray in the synagogues and on the street corners, in order to be seen by men. Truly I say to you, they have their reward in full."

Standing in the same temple court that day was a man without pretension. As a tax–gatherer, his name was synonymous with cheater, traitor, and selling out. The taxgatherers of the time of Christ made their living not only by collecting for the hated occupying government of Rome, but they made a clear profit by adding a percentage on the fee for themselves. Despised and rejected, this man could offer no litany of religious accomplishment to recommend himself to God. The only thing he had to offer was a broken heart and a humble plea for mercy. "God, be merciful to me, the sinner!"

How did God respond to this prayer? God didn't help the one who helped himself; He helped the helpless. "This man went down to his house justified rather than the other; for everyone who exalts himself shall be humbled, but he who humbles himself shall be exalted."

The View from the Pew

The book of Revelation has increasingly become the focus of interest in the New Testament. Hold a seminar on the book of Corinthians, and you'll attract the faithful few; publicize an in–depth study of Revelation, and you can guarantee a crowd. People have a consuming interest in the predicted future of planet earth. However, Revelation contains more than a glimpse into tomorrow; in its pages we can also clearly see today.

The book begins with a series of seven letters, dictated by Christ to seven churches in Asia minor. These churches contained strengths and weaknesses representative of Christian groups through time. The final letter, to the church at Laodicea, was to a gathering of believers suffering from "Ben Franklin's disease," a raging case of spiritual self–sufficiency.

> *And to the angel of the church in Laodicea write: The Amen, the faithful and true Witness, the Beginning of the creation of God, says this: "I know your deeds, that you are neither cold nor hot; I would that you were cold or hot. So because you are lukewarm, and neither hot nor cold, I will spit you out of My mouth. Because you say, 'I am rich, and have become wealthy, and have need of nothing,' and you do not know that you are wretched and miserable and poor and blind and naked, I advise you to buy from Me gold refined by fire, that you may become rich, and white garments, that you might clothe yourself, and that the shame of your nakedness may not be revealed; and eyesalve to anoint your eyes, that you may see. Those whom I love, I reprove and discipline; be zealous therefore, and repent"* (Rev. 3:14–19).

The Laodiceans knew all about helping themselves. Located in one of the most affluent cities of the Roman

Empire, the church thrived materially, and the people believed their prosperity to be a divine pat on the back. Yet from God's point of view the self–sufficiency their wealth had generated had devastated them.

The More Things Change...

The parallels between the conditions in Laodicea and the current state of much of the church in the West are significant. The religious scandals of our day attest to the effectiveness of a tried and true recipe for spiritual destruction:

- Poor boy makes good (the backwoods preacher gains national exposure)
- Poor boy gets the goods (the material rewards of the mass media make solid gold shower fixtures and an airconditioned dog house seem more and more appropriate)
- Poor boy with the goods gets up to no good ("I won't get caught. God needs me on His team!")
- Poor boy with the goods, up to no good, makes good ratings on "Nightline."

The hard–bitten atheist, the Pharisee and the tax gatherer, and the church in Laodicea (or Louisiana, for that matter), all illustrate an inescapable spiritual reality: people are in desperate need of God's help. When we live our lives independently of that help we court disaster.

A Sticky Point

Remember the first time you wanted to "do it yourself"? Face–to–face with an adult–sized challenge (like assembling a plastic B–52 model without dumping airplane glue all over the carpet) we convinced ourselves that we could handle the project alone. We glanced at the picture on the box and thought, "How complicated could this be?" Well–intentioned remarks like, "Are you sure you're ready for this?" or "Could you use a hand?" from some condescending adult sealed our decision. With a sneer of disgust we replied, "What do you think I am, some helpless little kid? Of course I can handle this!"

Then we'd open the box. The sight of eighteen million plastic parts and instructions the length of the average Tolstoy novel seemed a little overwhelming, but we plunged boldly on. We didn't need anyone's help. We'd show 'em.

You know the rest of the story. By the time we tried to "interface strut DD with tab Q" our hands, our desk, Mom's carpet, and even Scruffy the dog were covered with glue. We had a throbbing, tension headache and were the proud creators of a plastic mutation that more closely resembled a quonset hut than a flying fortress.

As I recollect my own personal battles with model airplanes and other do–it–yourself projects, a simple yet profound lesson seems to emerge. I could have saved myself hours of aggravation and frustration if I had simply had the wisdom to realize my own limitations and the humility to ask for a hand. But whether we are a ten–year–old agonizing over a model, or a fifty–year–old agonizing over a frustrating search for meaning and purpose in life, the answer to our struggle remains the same. We must look to a higher perspective. The answer does not lie in ourselves. As the brilliant French philosopher Pascal observed, "It is vain, O men, that you seek within yourselves the cure for your miseries. All your insight only leads you to the knowledge that it is not in yourselves that you will discover the true and the good."

Help for the Helpless

If a relationship with God isn't a question of trying harder, punctuating our lives with a set of outwardly impressive religious obligations and rituals, or seeking false comfort through amassing wealth or reputation, what is it all about? If the traditional American way to spiritual fulfillment doesn't work, is there an alternative?

Yes. The Bible calls it grace. Unearned, unmerited favor before God. Paul describes the nuts and bolts of grace in Romans 5:6–8: "For while we were still helpless, at the right time Christ died for the ungodly. For one will hardly die for a righteous man; though perhaps for the good man someone would dare even to die. But God demonstrates His own love toward us, in that while we were yet sinners, Christ died for us."

The Bible states that Christ did something for us that we were incapable of doing for ourselves. He died, not as a symbolic act or as an example of innocent suffering, but under the penalty for your wrongs and my wrongs. He paid the just price for our rebellious war of independence from God. Jesus made it possible for you and me to leave behind our deep inner loneliness and be restored to a right relationship with our Creator. A life of true fulfillment is possible only if we abandon our proud rationalizations and humbly receive the spiritual help that God freely offers and we so desperately need.

A View from Space

The world held its breath. The snowy, shadowy images appeared on television screens from Detroit to Djakarta. For the first time, mankind had slipped the bonds of earth and arrived safely on the alien soil of the moon. The message all humanity waited for made its way back some 220,000 miles to earth, "Tranquility Base here. The Eagle has landed."

Apollo 11 was a tribute to modern technology: No foul–ups; no glitches. Man had accomplished the impossible and had done so without a hitch. In fact Apollo missions 11 and 12 were so error–free they seemed almost routine. The world resumed breathing. The television ratings for moonwalks began to decline. When Apollo 13 lifted off from the Kennedy Launch Center, the mood of anxious anticipation had given way to a sense of smug certainty. We've done this before, and we will do it again.

On April 11, 1970, Apollo 13 entered earth orbit, shed the remnants of its Saturn 5 booster rocket, and shot away toward its silent silver destination. Everything was "A–O.K."

Days after launch, an unscheduled, understated message crackled over the Mission Control loudspeakers. The calm voice of flight commander James Lovell observed matter–of–factly, "Houston... We've got a problem."

And what a problem it was. An oxygen tank on the outside of the service module had ruptured, severely damaging the craft. The bad news poured in. First, the moon mission itself was scrubbed. Apollo 13 would have to fire its retro–rockets and return to earth. As the damage was surveyed, it became apparent that the command module could not supply the energy and air to sustain the three crew members through to re–entry. They would have to climb into the lunar lander and use its supplies to survive.

Then, the most sobering development of all. Because of the radically altered course back to earth, Apollo 13's return home would be limited to a very precise and narrow path. Missing the painfully small re–entry window meant catastrophe. If the craft came in too steeply, it would incinerate like a falling star. If the angle of attack was too high, the command module would skip off the atmosphere like a smooth stone on a calm lake. There would not be enough fuel or oxygen for a second chance.

What would you have done had you been in James Lovell's shoes? In Houston, scores of the brightest and best scientific minds were hard at work calculating, planning, anticipating every contingency. More than guess work, hunches, and the old college try were required to bring the crippled craft home. But, on the other hand, the Apollo 13 crew was well–trained and experienced. As test pilots they had encountered life and death situations before. The astronauts were faced with a clear choice; they could rely on the vast resources of ground control, or give it their best shot, on their own initiative, and hope for the best.

Apollo 13 managed to thread that crucial re–entry needle. Rather than swallowing hard and trying to be self–sufficient, James Lovell and crew meticulously heeded instructions from Mission Control. Tragedy was averted because the astronauts trusted a perspective greater than their own. Dependency, invested in the right place, saw them home safely and in one piece.

Our lives are no different. Like Apollo 13, we've "got a problem." As we have seen previously, there is a painfully narrow path to a right relationship with God. As our lives speed on, we approach our moment of truth. The question each of us must ask is, "Who is guiding me home?" The answer to our question is the difference between triumph and tragedy. God doesn't help those who help themselves. He helps those who have come to realize that, when they face the final curtain, they are helpless.

Please understand what the Bible teaches in this controversial area. By stating that God helps the helpless, Scripture doesn't advocate a passive, inert, "woe–is–me" approach to life. God has granted each of us tremendous gifts of talent, ability, and reason. He expects us to use and develop these gifts to their fullest capacity. But without God's mercy, without His unmerited favor, we will ultimately come up short.

A Trip to Paradise

Imagine yourself taking part in a sailboat race from Los Angeles to Honolulu. You have devoted the last five years of your life to training physically and developing your sailing skills just to participate in this competition. You are now more than ready to cover the distance. You have prepared for every possible contingency. The race will be a piece of cake. Nothing will keep you from your moment of glory in Hawaii.

Then the unexpected happens. Six hundred miles from the finish line you encounter a violent storm. Your boat suffers severe damage and eventually goes down. Much to your surprise you find yourself treading water in the middle of the Pacific ocean.

Suddenly on the horizon, a rescue ship appears. It draws nearer and nearer, and one of the crew on deck spots you as you bob on the waves like a waterlogged cork. They toss you a life preserver and tell you to hang on until they can draw you in to safety.

Would you push the life preserver away and yell, "No thanks. My goal is to make it to Hawaii alone, and I'll make it by myself. I'll swim the six hundred miles!"?

Insanity? The height of arrogance and pride? Perhaps. But not much different than the way millions of people are trying to make it to paradise today. The first step toward salvation is realizing that we are in over our heads. We cannot "help ourselves." The distance between heaven and us is far too great to make it on our own.

But all is not lost. God has accomplished the greatest rescue mission of all time. He has thrown us the spiritual life preserver of forgiveness made available by the death and resurrection of Jesus. As we find ourselves adrift in the ocean of life, we face an all–important choice; will we acknowledge our helplessness and take hold of God's mercy? Or will we just keep swimming?

Discussion   Questions

1. Read Romans 5:6–11. Do most people believe that Jesus died for us when we were at our worst? If someone told you God only loves religious people, how would you respond?

2. Many believe we can make it to heaven with a little help from the "man upstairs." What kind of help do you think you would need to make it to heaven?

3. Read Revelation 3:14–19. How do you suppose the people in that church reacted when they read Jesus' letter? If Jesus sent you a letter on the condition of your heart, what would it say?

CHAPTER VII
BUT WILL IT PLAY
IN PEORIA

*It ain't those parts of the Bible that I can't
understand that bother me, it is the parts I do
understand.*

— Mark Twain —

SOME CALL it advertising. Some call it public relations. Some call it out–and–out deception and fraud. But in our media–saturated, spectacle–jaded culture, many call it a necessity. I refer to one of the most pervasive forms of creative thinking in America today, the fine art of hype.

If a hall of fame for hype is ever put together, we can anticipate seeing some very familiar faces among its ranks. P. T. Barnum (of "There's a sucker born every minute" fame) will undoubtedly be honored. Bill Veeck, the baseball owner who brought the sport its first midget (Eddie Gaedell) as well as the infamous "Disco Demolition" riot at Comiskey Park in Chicago, will find a spacious niche carved out in tribute. Perhaps there will even be a shrine to fight promoter Don King's hair. But if such a museum is ever constructed, a large share of floor space should be devoted to the life's work of a man whose very name captures the essence of the subtle art of promotion, "Unswerving" Irving Rudd.

"Unswerving" Irving began his illustrious career as a publicist for the Brooklyn Dodgers. As he discovered his innate ability to make mountains out of mole hills, he branched out into other fields, most notably boxing and horse racing. "Unswerving" Irving was responsible for such great moments in hype as:

- Intentionally misspelling the huge sign welcoming patrons to the Yonkers Raceway. On a brilliant, spur–of–the–moment hunch, Rudd gave orders to a painting crew to render *Raceway*, *Racewya* instead. This planned error resulted in a deluge of free publicity for the track as every newspaper in New York ran large photos of the gaffe.
- The case of the "Bionic Fist." Rudd persuaded the manager of a heavyweight fighter to protest a planned bout when it was revealed that his opponent had undergone surgery to implant eight metal pins in his hand and to fuse smashed bones. The story of the boxer with the "Bionic Fist" was carried by papers all over the globe. As Rudd astutely observed, "Advertising can be very effective, but it's still only an ad. If a guy picks up a newspaper and reads a story about a boxer with a bionic fist, it becomes a real situation in his mind."

Strange? You bet. But the "best" was yet to come. The most bizzare highlight of "Unswerving" Irving's career came when he got involved in the 1981 World Boxing Association Junior Middleweight championship fight between Sugar Ray Leonard and a Ugandan boxer named Auyub Kalule. Bruce Newman, writing in *Sports Illustrated*, recounts that Rudd sought out the services of a Ugandan Witch doctor to bring a little color to the proceedings.

"I called the Ugandan mission and asked if they had any witch doctors," he (Rudd) says. The mission sent Ben Mugimba, whom Rudd identified for the press as a medicine man from Uganda. "This guy from Uganda was the goods," insists Rudd, who does concede that to help make ends meet during the slack

season for medicine men, Mugimba "ran a Gulf station in Kinshasa." Which is in Zaire, by the way. Rudd dressed Mugimba up in a ceremonial headdress and robe for what would be his first news conference, if you didn't count interviews after the occasional filling station hold up. Mugimba chanted. Mugimba swung a chicken over his head. Mugimba was hexing away with impressive verve when a radio reporter named Rock Newman jumped to his feet and stormed angrily out of the room, dismissing the demonstration as a farce that promoted racism. On the way back to his hotel room, Newman was attacked by a huge crow that pecked violently at his head. To escape the crazed bird, he was finally forced to leap, fully clothed, into a hotel swimming pool.[15]

Let's face it, hype is the order of the day. From watching Michael Jackson's hair catch on fire during the filming of a Pepsi ad to the "Spectacular 3–D SuperBowl Halftime Magic Show" (featuring no less an entertainer than the world renowned magician "Elvis Presto"), we have just about seen it all. As Americans we are unqualified experts on hype. When it comes to exaggerated claims, outlandish stunts, and desperate attempts to make something look better than it is, we know it and, most of the time, we love it.

With this in mind, let's consider two statements that many people would place in a special display, right next to the "Unswerving" Irving Shrine, in the Hall O' Hype. "All Scripture is inspired by God and profitable for teaching, for reproof, for correction, for training in righteousness; that the man of God may be adequate, equipped for every good work" (2 Tim. 3:16–17).

Taking a closer look at this statement unveils some startling facts. The word rendered "inspired" in the New American Standard Bible is the Greek term "theopneustos." Literally, this could be translated "God–breathed." The implication of point the apostle Paul conveys in this passage is eye–opening. To paraphrase, 2 Timothy 3:16–17 claims that the Bible is the very Word of God. We may have the same level of confidence that we are hearing God speak when we turn to Scripture as if we had stood in His presence and felt the very air of His breath as the words were spoken. Every Scripture, according to Paul, shares that level of inspiration. Every Scripture is "God–breathed."

Our second statement comes from no less a source than Jesus Christ Himself. "Do not think I came to abolish the Law or the Prophets; I did not come to abolish, but to fulfill. For truly I say to you, until heaven and earth pass away, not the smallest letter or stroke shall pass away from the Law, until all is accomplished" (Matt. 5:17–18).

The extent of Christ's claim is also striking. When He refers to the "smallest letter" in this passage, Jesus is making reference to the Hebrew yodh, which resembles our English apostrophe. The "stroke" Christ mentions is a tiny extension in Hebrew lettering called a serif. A serif makes the subtle, yet significant difference between almost identical looking letters. It is similar to the tiny line that distinguishes the capital letter E from an F. In essence what Jesus is saying is, "Not one apostrophe, not one distinguishing line between letters will be removed from the Bible until this whole world passes away. Down to the dotting of the i's and the crossing of the t's the Bible is the very word of God."

But Will It Play in Peoria?

The Bible claims to be divinely inspired, so much so that it is the very breathed word of God Himself, down to the last jot and tittle. These kinds of statements go over well in a church setting, but out in the world at large it's a different story. Thomas Henry Huxley spoke for many when he observed, "The doctrine of the infallibility of the Bible is no more self–evident than is that of the infallibility of the popes." *Time* magazine reports the existence of "a self–appointed supreme court of professors known as the Jesus Seminar, which meets twice a year to cast ballots on whether each of the Master's New Testament sayings is authentic or not. Sample conclusion: Jesus did say 'Blessed are the poor' but not 'Blessed are the meek' or 'Blessed are the peacemakers,' phrases that, the group contends, were added by the Gospel authors in an echo of Old Testament writings."[16]

Huxley and the "Jesus Seminar" are certainly not alone in their skepticism. Many dispute the Bible's claim of divine inspiration. To them, the Bible's extraordinary claim of God as its ultimate author is not too far removed from bringing in a witch doctor to promote a fight. Both are quite simply an exercise in hype.

When any issue draws such divergent points of view, we can reasonably anticipate some serious conflict and sharp verbal confrontation; but when the issue is as emotionally charged as is a discussion of the very credibility of the Bible, we can expect some real fire works.

And in this Corner...

I personally encountered the considerable heat of this debate sitting behind the rather imposing looking microphone of a Los Angeles radio station. As the Protestant spokesman on a late night phone–in religious talk show, I had said some controversial things before, but this one took the cake.

The rabbi and the Catholic priest who shared the panel with me looked shocked. The emcee of the program, who always loved a good brouhaha, had an expression of bewildered amusement on his face. The lights on the in–studio phone began to flash and wink like a Times Square billboard on New Year's Eve. That did it. I'd really stirred up a hornet's nest this time. The host cleared his throat and ventured out, "So, Pastor Richards... you actually believe that the Bible is to be taken literally? That, for instance, the first eleven chapters of Genesis are historical, not symbolic?"

There was a weighty moment of silence as I collected my thoughts and tried for the life of me to figure out what I had said to cause such unabashed embarrassment and delight.

I replied, "Yes. As a piece of literature the Bible must be interpreted literally. As for Genesis 1–11, the text is clearly historical in form and intent. It tells us the facts about our shared beginnings. The burden of proof lies with those who insist we suspend normal rules of interpretation and call this symbolism."

As you can guess, there was no shortage of calls, controversy, and conflict that cold winter evening. Few subjects have generated more heated debate in history than Old and New Testament Scripture, particularly when they are treated seriously.

Some well–meaning Christians try to dodge such a confrontational approach by "softening" the issue. "Sure the Bible claims to be divinely inspired, and sure there are some parts of it that are tough to reconcile with our sophisticated modern thinking. But, listen, we don't have to believe all the particulars. You know, the embarrassing parts like miracles reported as history, or statements that just don't happen to line up with our contemporary world view. Don't worry about those, just buy into the greater truths, the big concepts. Just believe that God is love and heaven is a wonderful place, and you'll be fine!"

But will we?

Danger: Breakdown Dead Ahead

This very popular school of thought runs headlong into two massive problems. First, we cannot separate the "big concepts" from the "particulars." The theological concepts of the Bible are built on specific and individual incidents and statements. If we don't buy the small points, how can we buy the large? We can easily find ourselves falling into a very common line of thinking, practiced by overly–enthusiastic, newly–licensed sixteen–year–olds at Honest John's Used Cars. The sensible parent usually suggests that a better investment of their son or daughter's life savings would be the serviceable '73 Volkswagen Super Beetle gathering dust in the corner of the lot. (The one with a motor that actually runs.) But it's far too late for common sense at this point. Junior has fallen hopelessly in love with a candy apple red convertible (whose odometer suspiciously reads 01123.4 miles). The time–honored cliche goes something like this: "Gosh Dad. I know the engine is a piece of junk, but just look at that outrageous body!" (This same kind of thinking has been responsible for more than one lousy marriage as well.) In theology, as well as in the used car buying game, the whole is but a sum total of the individual parts.

Second, if we can't trust the Bible on physical, historical matters that we can see and verify here on planet Earth, why trust it on spiritual, heavenly matters that are just a shade out of reach for ordinary mortals like you and me? As Jesus Himself pointedly questioned in John 3:12, "If I told you earthly things and you do not believe, how shall you believe if I tell you heavenly things?"

We are left with a compelling set of alternatives. Either the Bible is the Word of God (and free from error) or it *isn't* (and is full of mistakes). Either we should believe it and live our lives by it, or we should reject it and relegate it to the classics shelf of the local library where it will gather the dust it deserves. When any book makes claims of such an extraordinary, uncompromising nature as the Bible, there is simply no neutral ground. Either the Bible is the greatest book ever written, or it's the greatest hoax and the greatest collection of delusions ever perpetrated.

The Prosecution

From the day Martin Luther nailed his ninety–five Theses to the door of the castle church in Wittenberg to the moment Clarence Darrow approached the bar in Tennessee, the Bible has found itself at the center of controversy. As Bernard Ramm put it, "No other book has been so chopped, knived, sifted, scrutinized, and vilified. What book on philosophy or religion or psychology or *belles lettres* of classical or modern times has been subject to such a mass attack as the Bible? With such venom and skepticism? With such thoroughness and erudition? Upon every chapter, line and tenet?" Love it or hate it, mankind has found it nearly impossible to be passively indifferent about the Bible.

Could you imagine what it would be like if this long–running controversy were brought to court to be settled? (What an episode of Perry Mason or L. A. Law that would make!) If we were to put the Bible on trial, the case for the prosecution would be familiar to many of us in the jury box. Our district attorney would rise from his seat, smile confidently, and introduce "Exhibit A" for concluding the Bible is a hoax—the demonstrable errors of Scripture.

"Ladies and gentlemen of the jury, we are privileged to have the opportunity to take part in an extraordinary judicial proceeding. The subject of our inquiry will not be the culpability or negligence of an individual or a corporation, but of a book. A book that has had a radical influence on the morality, world view, even the very lives of countless individuals. The question at hand is, does this book, the Holy Bible, have a right to such influence? Can it rightly claim divine inspiration, or are its errors and inconsistencies so patent, so palpable, so obvious that it must, in the public interest, be publically exposed and discarded? It will be the purpose of the prosecution to demonstrate that this is the case. The facts will show that the Bible is guilty of errors in three essential categories that clearly disqualify it from being considered the 'Word of God.'"

Errors of Fact

"I submit for your consideration, the case of Judas Iscariot. Matthew the tax collector, who has been represented as an eyewitness of the events, describes Judas's demise in this manner: 'Then when Judas, who had betrayed Him, saw that He had been condemned, he felt remorse and returned the thirty pieces of silver to the chief priests and elders, saying, "I have sinned by betraying innocent blood." But they said, "What is that to us? See to that yourself!" And he threw the pieces of silver into the sanctuary and departed; and he went away and hanged himself' (Matt. 27:3–5).

"Judas was an apostle, one of the original twelve. We would expect that the biblical authors could get their facts straight on the death of this notorious individual. Yet in the book of Acts, Dr. Luke paints a different picture.

"He says, 'Now this man acquired a field with the price of his wickedness; and falling headlong, he burst open in the middle and all his bowels gushed out' (Acts 1:18).

"What was the cause of death, ladies and gentlemen? Was it hanging or disemboweling? Clearly we see contradictory statements of fact."

Errors of Harmony

Our D.A. continues his summation. "Ladies and gentlemen of the jury, some have pointed to the Bible as a source of great spiritual insight and wisdom. But with the unblinking eye of modern scholarship, we can determine that the Bible hopelessly contradicts itself in even its most elemental teachings.

"Moses, in the Old Testament book of Exodus, laid down a most exacting standard of justice. 'But if there is any further injury, then you shall appoint as a penalty life for life, eye for eye, tooth for tooth, hand for hand, foot for foot, burn for burn, wound for wound, bruise for bruise' (Ex. 21:23–25). A simple standard isn't it? Difficult to confuse or misinterpret.

"How then are we to take the equally famous words of Jesus Christ? In Matthew 5:38–39 He stated, 'You have heard that it was said, "An eye for an eye, and a tooth for a tooth." But I say to you, do not resist him who is evil; but whoever slaps you on your right cheek, turn to him the other also.'

"Which do we practice? Justice or mercy? Passivity or aggression? To forgive or get even? Another hopeless contradiction."

Errors of Philosophy

"Ladies and gentlemen of the jury, we live in the twentieth century. Living in this modern era has rendered certain ideas of the past obsolete. We now know that the world isn't flat, that raindrops aren't angel tears, and that the world doesn't rest on the shoulders of a giant.

"Beloved as it is, the Bible contains records of events that we know today are just as impossible. Babies are not born to virgins. Men do not walk on water. The dead do not return to life. Oh, certainly there was a time when people were naive and superstitious enough to believe such things, but those things are long past.

"The case appears open and shut. The facts are in. Ladies and gentlemen of the jury, as intelligent people we can come to only one conclusion, one verdict. The Bible is a quaint collection of myths and errors and native folklore from a primitive people. Nothing more."

Feeling quite pleased and confident, our prosecutor smiles, unbuttons his jacket, and serenely strides back to his seat. Case closed.

The Defense

At this point the presiding judge would nod to the counsel for the defense. Rising from his seat, he begins his closing remarks.

"Ladies and gentlemen of the jury. You have just heard some very familiar disputes of the Bible's claim to divine inspiration. These accusations are repeated whenever men gather to consider ultimate truth, from the ivory tower of the university to the dinette counter of a truck stop on Interstate 10. These disputes are familiar, and in a superficial sense they are powerful, but the question we must answer is, do they hold water?"

The Answers of Fact

"The prosecution has cited the death of Judas Iscariot as a glaring example of the hopeless contradictions of fact within the Bible. At first glance, it appears that we do have a problem. As the prosecution has pointed out, Matthew 27 does state that Judas did in fact hang himself, and Acts chapter 1 does present a graphic description of disemboweling. Yet before we blow the whistle and cry 'Hopeless contradiction!' we must ask in all fairness, are both actions possible at once?

"Matthew tells us that Judas, overwhelmed with remorse, threw his thirty pieces of silver into the temple sanctuary and bolted out to commit suicide by hanging. Jerusalem is a place of sharp precipice and jutting rocks. It is well within the bounds of possibility that Judas selected a tree on the side of one of the sharp, jagged hills to end his life. It is well within the bounds of possibility that the body hung long enough to begin the process of decomposition. It is well within the bounds of possibility that after a time, the rope or branch gave way causing the body to fall on to the rocks below. It is well within the bounds of possibility that the impact from such a fall would result in the mutilation of the corpse.

"If we were to interview a coroner of the time, and ask him to establish the cause of death, he might have pointed to rope burns around the neck and answered, 'Clearly this man hung himself.'

"But if we were to view the remains another question would arise. 'Doctor,' we might ask, 'what happened to Judas's midsection?' The doctor might well reply, 'As you can see, his midsection burst asunder.'

"'But wait doctor,' we might pursue, 'I thought you said that this man hung himself?'

'Yes. He certainly did.'

'But doctor, didn't you just say he was disemboweled?'

'Yes. That is true as well.'

"Would we demand that the doctor turn in his license for issuing a contradictory report on this gruesome death? No, we would commend him for the thoroughness of his investigation.

Ladies and gentlemen of the jury, can we offer any less commendation to the writers of Scripture? Matthew and Luke have faithfully and accurately given us a comprehensive picture of an unpleasant incident in the history of the first–century church. Far from a hopeless contradiction, these men have simply provided additional detail. There is no reason to cry contradiction here or, dare we say it, anywhere in the pages of Holy Writ. In the words of the 1987 report, *The Historical Reliability of the Gospels,* an international panel of thirty–four biblical scholars concluded, 'It is fair to say that all the alleged inconsistencies among the Gospels have received at least plausible resolutions.'"[17]

The Answers of Harmony

The defense attorney continues his rebuttal, "Ladies and gentlemen, popular thought and the prosecution have also alleged that the Bible is guilty of schizophrenic doctrine. They state that the commandments 'An eye for an eye' and 'turn the other cheek' can no more be reconciled than the notion of dry water or kosher pork. Is this the truth, or another case of jumping to conclusions without considering the facts?

"The prosecution is entirely correct in its quotation of Exodus 21:23–25. It does in fact lay down an easily understandable and applicable standard of justice, 'eye for eye, tooth for tooth, hand for hand, foot for foot, burn for burn, wound for wound, bruise for bruise.' But let's consider these remarks in context. In Exodus, Moses is relaying the *civil laws* that will govern their nation from God to an entire people. Jesus, in Matthew 5:39 is laying down a standard of *personal conduct* for individuals. Seeing these standards *in context* is absolutely essential to understanding their intent.

"Biblical scholar Dr. Gleason Archer underscores the importance of context in this issue:

> *If Matthew 5:39 applied to the state and to human government, then the principle of "Resist not evil" would mean the abolition of all law enforcement. There would neither be police officers nor judges nor prisons of any kind. All society would immediately fall prey to the lawless and criminal elements in society, and the result would be total anarchy. Nothing could have been further from Christ's mind than such Satan-glorifying savagery and brutality.*[18]

"Some would protest that having one code of conduct for individuals and another for civil authority indicates a double standard, giving too much power to government above the rights and prerogatives of its citizens. But that is a so-called double standard you and I willingly and gladly accept. For the police force to apprehend a thief and the criminal justice system to sentence and imprison him is justice. For you or I to apprehend a thief and lock him under our house indefinitely is to act as a vigilante and a kidnapper. Government privilege and personal privilege are clearly two different matters. The Bible merely recognizes this fact. Concerning the legal system of the nation Israel, justice and retribution for personal injury were to be swift and sure. But Jesus clarifies His desires for the personal conduct of citizens of the kingdom of God. Then, as now, individual Christian behavior is to be characterized by mercy and forgiveness in the face of evil."

The Answers of Philosophy

"The prosecution has also alleged that the view of reality contained in the pages of Scripture is completely at odds and unacceptable in the brave new world of the late twentieth century. And, let's face it, the Bible does contain a preponderance of examples of ordinary people encountering the extraordinary, the supernatural, yes, the miraculous. The question we must answer is, 'Can a modern, thinking individual accept such things without checking their intellect at the door?'

"To answer this question we must first acknowledge who we are dealing with when we open the Bible. The Christian perspective sums up and answers our problem of philosophy aptly:

> *The basis for believing in the miraculous goes back to the biblical conception of God. The very first verse of the Bible decides the issue. "In the beginning God created the heavens and the earth." (Genesis 1:1) If this verse can be accepted at face value, that in the beginning an infinite, personal God created the universe, then the rest should not be a problem. If He has the ability to do this, then a virgin birth, walking on water, feeding 5000 people with a few loaves and fish, and the other biblical miracles, become not only possible but expected.*[19]

"Ironically, the New Testament finds itself in a no–win situation. The religious leaders of Jesus' day refused to believe His claim to be God unless He would perform a spectacular sign. The modern thinker of today refuses to accept His claim because He did in fact do miraculous things. Is this a reasonable objection?"

The Clincher

"Ladies and gentlemen, to this point we have established that the Bible can stand up very well under tough scrutiny. As Martin Luther once observed:

> *Mighty potentates have raged against this book, and sought to destroy and uproot it—Alexander the Great and princes of Egypt and Babylon, the monarchs of Persia, of Greece and of Rome, the emperors Julius and Augustus—but they prevailed nothing. They are gone while the book remains, and it will remain forever and ever, perfect and entire, as it was declared at first. Who has thus helped it—who protected it against such mighty forces? No one, surely, but God Himself, who is master of all things.*

"Yet merely establishing that the Bible is a consistent book, and a reliable book, and a durable book does not provide the compelling evidence that it is a supernatural book, the very Word of God itself.

"But I submit to you that such compelling evidence does exist. And if this evidence is considered fairly by an honest seeker of truth, he or she will come to the conclusion that the Bible is the Word of God as well. The evidence I refer to is the startling phenomena of biblical prophecy.

"In the book of Isaiah the Bible makes a remarkable challenge: 'Remember the former things long past, For I am God, and there is no other; I am God, and there is no one like Me, Declaring the end from the beginning and from ancient times things which have not been done, Saying, "My purpose will be established, And I will accomplish all My good pleasure' (Isa. 46:9–10).

"In short, the Bible claims to be authored by God who lives beyond the limitations of time. Its author also claims to be in complete control of all events to ensure that the predictions of the future come to pass down to the smallest detail. The truth of this claim can be verified in the objective evidence of fulfilled predictive prophecy.

"Biblical researchers Josh McDowell and Don Stewart sum up a stunning example of this unmistakably supernatural phenomenon in the prophecy of King Cyrus found in Isaiah 44:28 and 45:1.

> *The prophet Isaiah, writing about 700 B.C., predicts Cyrus by name as the king who will say to Jerusalem that it shall be built and that the temple foundation shall be laid. At the time of Isaiah's writing, the city of Jerusalem was fully built and the entire temple was standing. Not until more than 100 years later would the city and the temple be destroyed by King Nebuchadnezzar in 586 B.C. After Jerusalem was taken by the Babylonians, it was conquered by the Persians in about 539 B.C. Shortly after that, a Persian king named Cyrus gave the decree to rebuild the temple in Jerusalem. This was around 160 years after the prophecy of Isaiah! Thus Isaiah predicted that a man named Cyrus, who would not be born for about 100 years, would give the command to rebuild the temple which was still standing in Isaiah's day and would not be destroyed for more than 100 years. This prophecy is truly amazing and is not isolated.[20]*

"McDowell and Stewart are quite right. The prophecy of the rise of King Cyrus is striking, but no more so than the vivid portrayal of the life, death, and resurrection of Christ found in Isaiah 53, or King David's agonizingly accurate foretelling of the crucifixion (a practice not yet invented during his time) in Psalm 22. Who enabled these ancient Hebrew prophets to see the future with such incredible clarity? Chance? Coincidence? A lucky guess? Or is it possible that these humble men were directly in touch with the Almighty?"

In Summation

"Ladies and gentlemen of the jury, I would like to conclude my remarks by disagreeing with the bold summation of the prosecution. The case against the Bible's extraordinary claim is not 'open and shut.' But to be honest, neither is the case for the divine inspiration of Scripture. We could settle this issue beyond doubt if somehow we could call the Author to the witness stand. But from what I understand, He normally doesn't respond to subpoenas, and we would also have a difficult time delivering the summons to appear.

"But even if the absolute convincing proof of God's physical presence may be lacking, may I suggest that He has certainly not left us without compelling, convincing evidence. God made us thinking beings, and as such He has left us more than enough data to satisfy the honest seeker of truth. He has left us a record of His appearance in human history. We can read what He said. We can see what He did.

"You will now retire to the jury room for your deliberations. With all due respect, the verdict you return, whether favorable or not, will matter little. Ultimate truth is decidedly unaffected by a majority vote.

"But I would suggest a greater deliberation must take place than behind the closed doors of a jury room. It is a deliberation that every man, woman, and child will have to make sooner or later. It is a deliberation that does not take place in the halls of justice, but in the courtroom of the human heart.

"The question at hand, in light of the consistency, history, and prophecy of the Bible, is simple and unmistakable: 'Will I believe God's message... or not?'"[21]

Meanwhile, Back in Iran

It is clear that God has indeed given us critical insight into the nature of life and reality in the pages of Scripture.

He has not been subtle in placing marks of divine inspiration in His Word. But for some the notion of a divine playbook in the game of life is unappealing. "Why should I look to God for guidance? I can get along fine all by myself!" But if we are honest, we must admit that sooner or later life throws a set of circumstances our way that begs for accurate, authoritative advice.

Consider the experience of Will Rodgers III. As captain of a ship in the U.S. naval task force stationed in the war torn waters of the Persian Gulf, tension had become a way of life. But on that stifling hot, hazy morning of July 4, 1988 the tension became explosive.

Rodgers' ship, the USS Vincennes, was drawn into combat when three Iranian gunboats fired at a U.S. helicopter. Within forty minutes the attackers were easily disabled. The battle would go down as another minor skirmish in an area of the world that has known precious little peace.

Then, suddenly, an unforeseen development occurred. The sophisticated radar aboard the Vincennes picked up a plane taking off from an airport that housed Iranian F–14 fighters. The radar blip was tracked as being directly on course for the missile cruiser, increasing in speed and beginning to descend. Repeated attempts to contact the mystery plane went unanswered. Automatic identification signals from the craft were monitored on a frequency usually used by the Iranian military.

Rodgers was on the hot seat. The ship's computers were cranking out volumes of information, most of it contradictory. The burning question at hand: To wait for clear confirmation or to fire at the potential threat? Rodgers remembered what hesitation had cost the crew of the USS Stark some months before. A crippled ship and a large number of casualties were a distinct possibility. His choices were stark and demanding: take action and risk an international incident, or hesitate and risk who knows how many casualties. One official noted that the captain had all of 240 seconds to weigh the pros and cons and act.

The rest is history. Captain Rodgers went with his gut level reaction and gave the order to fire. Two surface–to–air missiles slammed into the side of a commercial Iran Air A–300 Airbus killing the 290 passengers and crew on board.

Will Rodgers III knows all about hard choices. In a message dispatched to his Persian Gulf commander he said, "This is a burden I will carry the rest of my life, but under the circumstances and considering all the information available to me at the moment, I took this action to defend my ship and crew."

What does the agonizing decision of a Navy commander have to do with accepting or rejecting the Bible as the Word of God? The parallels are striking. Sooner or later we will all face our own personal moment of truth. Granted our moment of truth may not happen on the bridge of a Navy missile cruiser, but at one time or another we will all face choices with life or death consequences. Choices that will decide not only the way a day, a month, or a year may go, but choices that will matter for all eternity. How will I face the afterlife? Do I really believe that Jesus is God? In the face of heart breaking tragedy, where will I find the strength to survive?

Like Captain Rodgers, we will find ourselves on the hot seat. And like Captain Rodgers we will be overwhelmed by seemingly contradictory information. At a time like that, who wouldn't want a completely reliable, trustworthy guide to turn to? Not the cold cranking of decimals and digits from some computer system. Not the well intentioned, but often wrong conclusions of conventional cracker barrel wisdom. Not a gut level hunch or a faith in feelings, but the very breathed Words of God, tried and true.

When your moment arrives, where will you turn?

Discussion Questions

1. Read II Timothy 3:16–17. Why do you suppose so many people have a hard time accepting the Bible as the Word of God?

2. Have you ever come across a passage of the Bible that disturbed you? What was it and why did it bother you?

3. When people face a difficult passage in the Bible, how do they react? What are some constructive ways to deal with difficult to understand verses?

4. Can you think of situations where our view of the Bible would have very practical impact on our lives? How important is it to have confidence in the truth of Scripture?

CHAPTER VIII
JESUS, LET'S DO LUNCH!

*But too many people now climb onto the cross
merely to be seen from a greater distance,
even if they have to trample somewhat on the
One who has been there so long.*

— Albert Camus —

NORMALLY A glance through the movie section of the local paper is as exciting and thought provoking as reading the soy bean futures section of the business page. But this Thursday evening edition was different, radically different. Splashed across an expensive two–full–page ad was the seemingly unanimous verdict of the working press.

**** HIGHEST RATING. THE FILM SUCCEEDS BRILLIANTLY.

—Marsha McCreadie, *Arizona Republic*

THERE'S A PRODIGIOUS GREATNESS ON DISPLAY HERE. IT'S A WORK OF GREAT SERIOUSNESS BY ONE OF THIS COUNTRY'S MOST GIFTED FILM–MAKERS. EVERYONE INTERESTED IN THE ART OF MOVIEMAKING SHOULD SEE THIS FILM.

—Hal Hinson, *Washington Post*

AN INTENSE, UTTERLY SINCERE, FREQUENTLY FASCINATING PIECE OF ART BY A DIRECTOR

144 Reasonable Doubts

FOR WHOM, CLEARLY, THE MESSAGE OF
JESUS' LIFE HAS IMMEDIACY AND MEANING.
—Sheila Benson, _Los Angeles Times_

But movie reviewers weren't the only ones commenting
on this extraordinary, newly released piece of commercial
art. Italian director Franco Zeffirelli called it "damaging to
the image of Christ. He cannot be made the subject of low
fantasies." Media pastor Jerry Falwell added, "Neither the
label 'fiction' nor the First Amendment gives Universal
(Pictures) the right to libel, slander and ridicule the most
central figure in world history." Bill Bright, founder and
head of Campus Crusade for Christ stated, "If I had that
film in my hand tonight, I would call together the leaders of
the Christian world and we would have a big bonfire
celebration."[22] Bright went so far as to offer to raise $10
million to pay for the film's production costs if all copies
would be destroyed.

Despite one of the largest and most vocal protests
against the release of any movie in recent memory, the
source of all this praise and anger, _The Last Temptation of
Christ_, has already come to a theater near you.

A Reason for Rage

Why all the fuss and controversy? To understand the
uproar over this two–and–a–half hour spectacle, it is
crucial to grasp the basics of the New Testament picture of
Jesus. In his biography of Christ, the apostle John states,
"In the beginning was the Word (Jesus), and the Word was
with God, and the Word was God.... And the Word
became flesh, and dwelt among us, and we beheld His
glory, glory as of the only begotten from the Father, full of
grace and truth" (John 1:1, 14). John asserts that Jesus was
God in human flesh, fully human and fully divine.

Another eyewitness, Simon Peter, shares his insight into
the moral character of Christ: "Christ also suffered for
you, leaving you an example for you to follow in His steps,
who committed no sin, nor was any deceit found in His

mouth; and while being reviled, He did not revile in return; while suffering He uttered no threats, but kept entrusting Himself to Him who judges righteously" (1 Pet. 2:21–23).

Was Peter qualified to give such an all–encompassing assessment? As Christ's disciple, he had been with Jesus day and night for over three years. He had seen how Jesus handled public applause and adulation, as well as scorn and rejection. He had seen how Jesus handled times of peace as well as times of crushing pressure.

His verdict? Jesus Christ was sinless, never failing to be God's ideal for man at any moment.

But perhaps the most telling testimony to the moral character of Jesus is found not in words, but in the silence of those who hated Him. In the eighth chapter of the book of John, Christ is confronted by the religious elite of His day. To a group of men who would eventually orchestrate His crucifixion, Jesus asked a question that was at once startling and challenging: "Which one of you convicts Me of sin? If I speak truth, why do you not believe Me?" (John 8:46).

What a wide open opportunity. In a public setting, with a largely undecided crowd hanging on every word, Jesus had literally teed up the ball for His detractors. This simple question was similar to a presidential candidate asking his opponent, "Why wouldn't you vote for me?"

The response?

Silence.

Even Christ's most committed enemies could find no departure from moral perfection in His life. As the promised Messiah, Jesus was not only 100 percent God and 100 percent man, his personal conduct was beyond even the microscopic reproach of those who rejected Him.

And Now for Something Completely Different

While the Jesus of the New Testament and orthodox Christianity through the ages is clear and unmistakable, Universal Pictures has presented a stunningly different portrayal. Director Martin Scorsese has churned out a movie version of Nikos Kazantzakis's book *The Last Temptation of Christ*. In harmony with the 1955 best selling novel, Scorsese's Jesus (played by actor Willem Dafoe) represents a disorienting departure from the Christ of history.

As *Time* magazine noted:

> *Scorsese presents the early Jesus as a weak and dithering collaborator who builds crosses used by the Romans to execute Jewish rebels. Later He becomes the wild-eyed guru to a band of ragged followers but remains apprehensive and fundamentally confused about his message and his mission. He persuades Judas, his best friend, to betray him to fulfill God's plan. During the reverie on the cross, Jesus is shown briefly having sex with his wife, Mary Magdalene. Later in the fantasy, after Magdalene dies, he weds Mary of the biblical duo Mary and Martha, then commits adultery with Martha…. In one grotesque scene, Jesus reaches into his chest (although it looks more like his belly), yanks out his heart and holds it up for his apostles to admire. At times Jesus sounds like a mumbling method actor (his first sermon begins 'Umm, uh, I'm sorry'), at others like a recent graduate of the Shirley MacLaine School of Theology ('Everything's a part of God').*[23]

Add to this Jesus' anguished comments, "I am a liar. I am a hypocrite. I am afraid of everything… Lucifer is inside me… " and even the most casual observer would admit we have a source of real and legitimate controversy. Even with the film's opening credit disclaimer that *Temptation* was based on Kazantzakis's fictional account and not the New

Testament, the use and distortion of historical names, places, and events lit the fuse of conflict.

Fuel on the Fire

To grasp the full implications of what Scorsese and Universal have produced, it's helpful to remove an emotional lightning rod like Christ from our consideration. Imagine a film version of the life of a modern personality with a few fictionalized moral failings thrown in to make the person more real. Imagine the reaction to a movie that portrayed John F. Kennedy as a child molester or Martin Luther King as a con man and a thief. In this light the size and passion of protest this film has received becomes more easily understandable.

Meanwhile... Back on the Talk Show Circuit

Perhaps the easiest way to determine if an issue has touched a nerve in our culture is not to do man on the street interviews or commission a Gallup Poll. We can simply consult the pages of the *TV Guide* and find out what Geraldo, Oprah, Phil, and Ted Koppel are featuring this week. From Morton Downey Jr. to Sally Jesse Raphael, *Temptation* garnered more than its share of the public airwaves.

During the height of the controversy, I was invited to be a part of a phone-in talk show to represent the point of view of those who objected to the film. As the program began, most callers were supportive and commended us for standing up for our beliefs. But I've sat in on enough of these sessions to know that sooner or later the praise will end and the proverbial other shoe will drop.

After discussing the relative merits of the movie and the value and character of the protests against it, the program took an interesting turn. As one caller put it, "You people disagree with Kazantzakis and Scorsese, but why should I believe the Bible's portrayal of Jesus?"

The nail had been hit on the head. The calls flooded in. "Hasn't the Bible been changed over the years?" "How do I know that the Bible isn't just a bunch of myths?" The callers had seized upon the crux of the issue. If the Bible isn't a reliable record of historical fact, then your guess, my guess, or Universal Pictures's guess about the actions, relationships, and character of Jesus Christ are all equally valid. *But* if the Bible is reliable history, we had better pay serious attention to its message.

Pass the Secret

One of the most popular and least challenged objections to the historicity of the New Testament view of Christ came up early in the program. A caller boldly asserted, "Everyone knows that the Bible has been changed hundreds and hundreds of times."

This point of view is often presented with a compelling illustration. At one time or another we have all attended a get–together where part of the entertainment was a rousing game of "Pass the Secret." The rules are very familiar. A line of people is formed, with the first person being given a complicated, often nonsensical message on a piece of paper. To start the game the first person reads the message to himself and whispers it into the ear of the next in line. The secret gets passed until the poor sap at the end of the line repeats the message out loud. Invariably, the message is so distorted that everyone has a big laugh and the person at the end swears that she will never play this stupid game again (or at least make sure she isn't stuck at the end of the line!). Interestingly, many people confidently believe that the message of the Bible has gone through a similar distortion over time. "Why, if Matthew, Mark, Luke, and John were here right now, they wouldn't even recognize what they wrote." Or so the argument goes.

Pass the Secret is a very vivid illustration of our tendency to be poor listeners, but does it maintain its validity as an accurate picture of how the Bible has been passed on over time?

Pass It On

If the Bible was passed ear to ear, this illustration might hold up, but is this the case? What is that book, gathering dust on coffee tables across America, based on?

No one claims to have the original manuscripts of the New Testament today, but that is no cause for alarm. Our record of the life and teaching of Jesus Christ is based on data from over 5,280 copies of the original text in the original language, Greek. Included in this body of data are pieces like the Rylands Fragment of the Gospel of John, dating back to 120 A.D. or less than forty years after the original was likely written.

We can add to this some translations of the New Testament into other ancient languages (like Aramaic and Latin) known to scholars as "versions." There are nearly eighteen thousand known examples of versions available to us today. Add to this the over eighty–six thousand New Testament verse citations in letters from early church officials to one another, and we have a huge body of corroborating evidence with which we can check our message.

When we examine these documents, and compare and contrast passage versus passage we are faced with some startling conclusions. Renowned New Testament scholar Dr. F. J. A. Hort summarized the reliability of the New Testament:

> *The proportion of words, virtually accepted on all hands as raised above doubt is very great; no less than seven–eighths of the whole. The remaining one–eighth formed in large part by changes of order and other comparative trivialities constitutes the whole area of criticism. We find that setting aside differences of orthography (spelling), the words in our opinion still subject to doubt make up about*

*one-sixtieth of the New Testament. In this
second estimate the proportion of
comparatively trivial variations is beyond
measure larger than in the former so that the
amount of what can in any sense be called
substantially a variation is but a small fraction
of the whole residuary variation, and can
hardly form more than one-one-thousandth
part of the entire text.*[24]

When we get down to brass tacks, the facts are
stunning. New Testament scholar Dr. Robert L. Thomas
said that if all seriously disputed New Testament verses
were compiled together, they would make up less than
one–half of a page of text. None of these variations cast a
doubt on the meaning of a verse, and no major doctrine of
historic Christianity is in question in any disputed text.

Time Out for a Rule Change

What can we determine from all this? If we are going to
use Pass the Secret as an illustration of how the Bible has
been handed down over time, we'll have to change the
rules of the game to fit the facts.

Instead of whispering our message ear–to–ear, let's have
each person write down the message as it is passed along.
Would reliability go up?

Instead of a nonsense message like "Dr. Huxtable, Theo
flushed a ham down the toilet," let's make our message so
important that each person in the game would be willing to
lay down his or her life to preserve it. Would reliability go
up?

Instead of forming one line of people, let's set up fifty–
five hundred lines of people committed to copying this
message in the original language. While we're at it, let's
also add eighteen thousand lines of bilingual people who
could accurately translate our message into other languages
as well. Would reliability go up?

Instead of having one person speak our message at the end of the game, let's collect the slips of paper our participants used to pass the word along. Let's have English and foreign language experts translate, compare, and contrast our evidence for message content. Would reliability go up?

Seems like overkill, doesn't it? The chances of substantially confusing our message would be so infinitesimally small that all the suspense would be removed from the game. Instead of Pass the Secret, our game would be better called Pass the Certainty. Surprise. This is an accurate parallel to the process our New Testament has gone through to get to us today. Quite a departure from the conventional view of a document torn to bits by half–understood oral traditions and corrupting, mad monks, isn't it?

As Dr. F. F. Bruce observed, "The evidence for our New Testament writings is ever so much greater than the evidence for many writings of classical authors, the authenticity of which no one dreams of questioning... If the New Testament were a collection of secular writings, their authenticity would be generally regarded as beyond all doubt."[25]

Mything the Point

For some, discovering that the Bible hasn't been changed and distorted over the years is interesting but unsatisfying. The callers to the talk show weren't going to let us off that easily. Another caller protested, "All right, so the Bible has been passed down to us accurately. But what if it is simply an accurate myth? How do we know that a bunch of bored Galilean fisherman didn't make the whole thing up while drying their nets one day?"

Many people have bought into this widely accepted dismissal of the life of Christ. After all, we weren't there, so who can know if it is true or not? Before we allow Jesus to get lost in this fog of agnosticism we owe it to ourselves and to intellectual honesty to ask, are there any compelling reasons to consider the biblical record as good history? The answers may surprise you.

The Literary Factor

As any survivor of Freshman English 101 knows, the first rule of accurate interpretation of any piece of literature is to allow the text to speak for itself. Violating this simple rule can have dire consequences. Imagine a student approaching Shakespeare's *Macbeth* with the preconceived notion that this classic stage production was really intended to be a cook book. ("See, right here on the first page. 'Boil, boil, toil and trouble. Fire burn and caldron bubble.' Clearly directions for temperature settings. And look at all the references to food. Forget all this stuff about 'Act I, Scene 3,' and the character names and stage direction. This was a cook book that later writers doctored up to look like a play.") Unless the professor gives credit for unusual perspective and creative writing, our student's grade point average will be on full life support by semester's end. Any accurate interpretation of Shakespeare begins by acknowledging the intent of the author, in this case to write a play.

The same common sense rule applies to any responsible view of the New Testament. What did its authors intend to write? The apostle John begins his first letter with this telling introduction: "What was from the beginning, what we have heard, what we have seen with our eyes, what we beheld and our hands handled, concerning the Word of Life" (I John 1:1). We could accurately paraphrase John as saying, "Our message about Jesus Christ is no fantasy. We speak to you about the One we saw with our own eyes. We heard the sound of His voice as He spoke. When we touched Him we felt the very warmth of His hand. Yet He is the eternal One, the very Word of Life."

Simon Peter, writing in his second letter, underscores the point: "For we did not follow cleverly devised tales when we made known to you the power and coming of our Lord Jesus Christ, but we were eyewitnesses of His majesty" (2 Peter 1:16). Clearly the original purpose of the New Testament writers was to present an accurate record of actual, historical facts and their meaning.

The Historical Factor

Don't tell me, let me guess. Racing through your mind right now is the next logical objection, "So what if the New Testament authors intended to write accurate history. The big issue is, Did they succeed in pulling it off?"

For many years this question would bring any discussion of biblical credibility to a screeching halt. It was a foregone conclusion that the Bible contained a host of unverifiable people, places, and events. In the early 1900s it was assumed that as the science of archeology progressed, the accuracy of the New Testament would be first called into question, and finally dismissed as well intentioned fiction.

Remarkably, the opposite has occurred. In the cover story "Who Was Jesus?," *Time* magazine noted:

> *Archeological finds have also added to the knowledge of New Testament happenings and brought new credence to Scripture. For example, an inscription unearthed in 1961 at Caesarea confirmed for the first time that Pilate was a 1st century Roman governor, as the Bible reports. More significantly, the Dead Sea Scrolls, discovered in 1947, demonstrate a deeply ingrained 1st century Jewish belief in a Messiah-like figure and the need for spiritual renewal—teachings that anticipate Christ's message. "After the Dead Sea Scrolls were discovered, you could no longer say there was no historical Jesus," says Theologian Otto Betz.*[26]

As the radio program progressed, another caller (a bit irate that we had the nerve to refer to Christ as an historical figure on a par with Lincoln or Kennedy)

confidently asserted, "Well, I *know* that there is no
historical record that Jesus even existed apart from what's
in the New Testament."

I replied, "I hate to contradict you, but your statement
simply doesn't hold water. Christ is clearly mentioned as a
bona fide historical figure in the writings of the Roman
historians Tacitus (in *Annals*) and Seutonius (*Life of
Claudius*). The real clincher is found in the Jewish historian
Josephus's *Antiquities*." Josephus wrote:

> *Now there was about this time Jesus, a wise
> man, if it be lawful to call him a man, for he
> was a doer of wonderful works, a teacher of
> such men as receive the truth with pleasure. He
> drew over to him both many of the Jews and
> many of the Gentiles. He was Christ, and when
> Pilate, at the suggestion of the principal men
> among us, had him condemned to the cross,
> those who loved him at first did not forsake
> him; for he appeared to them alive again the
> third day; as the divine prophets foretold these
> and ten thousand other wonderful things
> concerning him. And the tribe of Christians so
> named for him are not extinct at this day.*[27]

It is clear that history and archeology strongly bolster
the credibility of the New Testament picture of Christ.

The Human Factor

Perhaps the most compelling reason to consider the
New Testament message historical and not mythical is
found in the lives of an all–too–human group of men called
the apostles. This ragtag conglomeration, ranging from
blue–collar fishermen to a white–collar executive with the
Roman IRS, shared a common experience. They were all
eyewitnesses of the life, death, and resurrection of Jesus
Christ.

Being vocal about such an experience in Roman–
occupied Palestine was no way to win a popularity
contest. Going public on the subject of a risen and living
Jesus meant for many a certain guarantee of immense

suffering, even death by no less a punishment than crucifixion.

Under these conditions, what could have motivated these men to boldly and publicly lay their lives on the line? We gain a remarkable insight into the thinking of the apostles in Acts 4:19–20. Hauled in before the same ruling council that had politically orchestrated the crucifixion of Christ, Peter and John were sternly warned to put a lid on their teaching. "But Peter and John answered and said to them, 'Whether it is right in the sight of God to give heed to you rather than to God, you be the judge; for we cannot stop speaking what we have seen and heard.'"

A place of mortal danger? Unquestionably. These very common men found their lives on the line. If these seasoned politicos were able to pressure the Roman governor to crucify a widely–known public figure like Christ, dispatching of these two nobodies would be short work indeed. Peter and John were clearly willing to die at this point, but not for a nice philosophy or a helpful way of life. They were willing to suffer any consequence that might come for stating what they had seen and heard.

This bold statement raises a difficult question for those who suppose that the life of Christ was a Galilean daydream. Why die for a known lie? Death was not only a risk for this group of men, but in the vast majority of cases it was a reality. Eleven out of the twelve apostles had their lives cut short in a brutal, grisly manner. In the majority of cases, all they had to do to stop the execution was to cave in, recant, and admit that the whole thing was a hoax.

None took the easy way out. They were convinced beyond a shadow of a doubt, by personal experience, that Jesus was the risen Messiah. They willingly chose death over denial.

Ad Nauseam

It is the evident courage, integrity, and conviction of the apostles that underscores a particularly inaccurate and offensive scene from *Temptation*. During the climactic dream sequence at the end of the film, Jesus is shown walking with His wives and children. He stops to listen to a man preaching at an open air gathering—none other than the apostle Paul. Paul is proclaiming the traditional New Testament message that Jesus of Nazareth was the Son of God, that He was tortured and crucified for our sins, and that three days later He rose from the dead. Jesus asks Paul if he ever saw Jesus of Nazareth. Paul replies, "No. But I saw a light." (Another inaccuracy—see 1 Corinthians 9:1.) Jesus then tells Paul that He is Jesus and asks why he is telling these people lies about Him. Paul tells Jesus to look around Him and see how unhappy the people are. Their only hope is a resurrected Jesus. They need God. "If I have to crucify you, I'll crucify you. If I have to resurrect you, I'll resurrect you. My Jesus is more important than you are. I'm glad I met you. Now I can forget about you."

The Paul of *Temptation* comes off as an amoral pragmatist who cared precious little about truth. In one short sequence the life of one of the most influential men in history is repainted as a cynical exercise in futility. The ethics of Paul, and by extension the rest of the apostles, are presented as totally situational (if not hypocritical), the message as merely a bandaid for bruised psyches, and the deaths of the martyrs as a meaningless commitment to a lie they fabricated. When we compare *Temptation* to reality, this "work of art" is not only a distortion of historical fact, but an assault on personal character.

It's Only Human Nature

At this point some people remark, "So the apostles died for their belief. What's the big deal? The fanatic in Beruit who loads up his Volvo with plastic explosives does the same thing. What's the difference? It doesn't prove that the fanatic's beliefs are true."

Yes, death for a belief doesn't make a belief true, but a martyr's death does indicate something about human nature that is crucial to grasp.

The battlefields of this world have seen some stunning examples of both bravery and futility. Few conflicts have embodied these characteristics more fully than the Iran/Iraq war of the 1980's. Iraq tended to favor a modernistic approach; use superior fire power and modern tactics, and victory should be assured sooner or later. Iran, on the other hand, embraced another strategy; it was called the "human wave." The practice was simple. Mass enough people together and send hundreds upon hundreds directly into enemy fire. Sooner or later the enemy runs out of ammunition, and those who are fortunate enough to be at the end of the line swarm to victory.

In the aftermath of these bloody skirmishes, a sobering discovery was made. In the pockets of the human wave volunteers were found white plastic keys. It was discovered that the keys represented something of crucial importance to the devout Shiite Moslems of Iran. Before battle these soldiers were told that if they laid down their lives in a Jihad or "holy war," they would be guaranteed a place in heaven. The simple, white piece of plastic was their own personal "key to the kingdom."

Why participate in a human wave assault? Why depart this world as a human detonator in a car bomb? The answer is simple; in both cases, the people honestly believed they were dying for the truth. No one signed up for human wave duty because they believed the Ayatollah Khoumeini was an unstable, fanatical crackpot. They died, willingly, because they were absolutely convinced they were dying not for a lie, fantasy, or nice philosophy, but for the truth.

The apostles died for the same commitment to truth but with an important difference. The human wave volunteer dies taking the word of an Iranian mullah. He has no first-hand knowledge. No deceased fellow soldier has come back to tell him, "Yes. This is really true. Follow orders and heaven is yours!" Our soldier takes his stand solely on the word of country and clergy. On the other hand, the apostles died for first–hand, experiential, observable truth. They explicitly claimed that they had seen Jesus alive after His death. They staked their lives that what they personally saw and heard was truly so. The authenticity of the New Testament account of the life, death, and resurrection of Jesus Christ is quite literally sealed in blood.

What sort of personality inspired the heroically sacrificial actions of the apostles? Was it the weak, uncertain, Hamlet–like Jesus of *Temptation*? Or the solid, certain, righteous, and loving Jesus of the Scriptures? Was it the Jesus who posed unanswerable questions? Or the Jesus who provided answers? Was it the Jesus who struggled through life? Or the Jesus who changed lives?

Writing in the *Jerusalem Post*, Emmy Award winning documentary filmmaker Pierre Sauvage offers this telling insight:

> *Righteousness, Last Temptation ultimately seems to say, lies merely in the experience of inner struggle, not in the joyous accomplishment of God's will. And that flies in the face of what I have come to know from some of Jesus' disciples, Christians who remained true to themselves and their beliefs at a time when Christian apostasy was running rampant in Nazi-occupied Europe.*
>
> *I'm alive today because even then, there were such true-life Christians. I've come to know them because I've just spent five years making a film about them—a Jewish film in praise of the people who welcomed me into the world. For it happens that I was born and sheltered in a mostly Huguenot community in the mountains of France: There, in and around the village of Le Chambon, some 5,000 Christians defied the Nazis and their French accomplices, taking in my parents and me, and some 5,000 other Jews. I learned there that there had been no*

great inner struggle. No agonized sleepless nights. No momentous debate over the Big Decision. You just did what you had to do. As if nothing else was possible. Without looking upon it as any big deal. Le Chambon took us in, as one Jewish refugee put it, because these Christians were "the most solid people on earth"—rooted in their families, rooted in their heritage, rooted in their land, rooted, yes, even in the Jewish roots of their faith... "By their fruits ye shall know them," said Jesus himself, according to Scripture. If he had anything to do with inspiring the actions of the good Christians of Le Chambon and others like them, he could not have been the tortured, rootless soul of The Last Temptation of Christ.[28]

Between a Rock and a Hard Place

When we consider the internal claims, the external evidence, and the absolute commitment of its authorship, the New Testament places the modern thinker in an uncomfortable position. As Peter Stuhlmacher of the University of Tubingen remarked, "As a Western Scripture scholar, I am inclined to doubt these (Gospel) stories, but as a historian I am obliged to take them as reliable. The biblical texts as they stand are the best hypothesis we have until now to explain what really happened."

The $64,000 Question

When traditional intellectual smokescreens begin to dissipate, the question of Christ comes increasingly into focus. At one point or another in our lives we will have to deal with this Jesus of Nazareth. He is unavoidable. He is unmistakable. His nearness is inevitable in the life of every human being. The question that remains to be answered is, What will we do with Jesus? How will we respond to Him?

The Response of Idolatry

An anonymous wit once observed, "In the beginning God made man in His own image and likeness... and ever since we've been returning the favor." This one–liner captures the essence of one of humanity's most time–honored and cherished traditions—idolatry. From Mesopotamia to Madison Avenue, we have consistently come to the conclusion that God is simply out of step with modern life. The Kingdom of Heaven's biggest problem lies in the realm of product development, packaging, and public relations. Perhaps all God really needs to get things rolling are a few small suggestions from religious experts like you and me. Can you imagine how a conversation between the Almighty and a modern–day ad man might go?

"God, sweetheart, so good to see you. We're really glad to have your business, but listen, we've got to talk. You see there's this problem. Nothing personal, mind you, but it's *You*. Now, we know that You're very concerned about the truth angle and all that stuff. Hey! We tried truth around here just last week... Real refreshing, a nice change of pace... But who can live with it? The average guy You're trying to reach prefers things, well, a little less complicated. That's it! Like this Trinity concept. Hey, we all know it's true, but who can understand it? Do You think we can simplify that a little? Oh, and while we're on the subject, how about this holiness issue. Our market research shows that Your standards are just a smidge too high. Hey, we know people here Lord, and let me tell You, they would be far more open if You asked for, say, a 32 percent commitment of their lives rather than 100 percent. That would leave them free for an occasional affair, R–rated movies, and an early tee time on Sundays. I know, I know. It's a little bit of a departure for You, but sleep on it, o.k.? Listen, it's been great to see You. Give Gabriel and the boys my best. Have Your service call my service and we'll do lunch..."

Far fetched? Maybe not. The nature of biblical worship is for humanity to approach God on His terms and to acknowledge His truth as He has revealed it, but a far different approach is in vogue today. If we don't like what God says, we edit it. If we don't like God's standards, we reserve the right to amend them. And if we don't happen to like who God is, we repackage Him in a more acceptable, more "relatable" form.

Temptation director Martin Scorsese captured the essence of the new idolatry when he stated, "What I've tried to create is a Jesus who, in a sense, is just like any other guy on the street. In his struggle to reach God and find God, he reflects all our struggles. I thought it would give us all hope." This is a nice statement with a fatal flaw. Can we "create" our own version of God without sacrificing truth? Can we find real hope in an edited, distorted, hence false messiah? Scorsese is correct in his observation that we all struggle with our separation from God, but is pulling Jesus down to our own desperate level the answer? To give the starving a picture of food, but not the real meal, hardly seems a public service.

How does all this relate to you and me? We must honestly ask ourselves a very difficult question: Have we come to Christ as He truly is? Or have we settled for the false comfort of a pliable messiah, incapable of offending us, incapable of challenging us, but also incapable of saving us? There is no comfort in a savior with feet made of clay.

The Response of Indifference

With all the furor *Temptation* has generated, many believe that there are only two possible perspectives on this movie. One can either be passionately behind this project or dead set against it, with precious little room for a neutral position. Unfortunately there is a third point of view that rarely grabs air time on the CBS Evening News. This camp's position is so inescapable and direct that it can be summed up in two words: Who Cares?

For many the turmoil over this film is an amusing side show. "Why get so worked up about a movie? I've got too much going on in my life to get hot and bothered about trivial religious issues."

To gain insight into why a few thousand feet of film have produced such a strong reaction, we must grasp a central truth of Christianity. To someone who believes in Christ, Jesus is God in human flesh, savior, role model, and teacher, but along with all of this, Jesus Christ is a personal friend. Jesus does not call His disciples to follow Him cringing in fear from afar, but to walk with Him in marvelous relationship of closeness and intimacy. Jesus said, "You are My friends, if you do what I command you. No longer do I call you slaves, for the slave does not know what his master is doing; but I have called you friends, for all the things that I have heard from My Father I have made known to you" (John 15:14).

With this truth in mind, the degree of emotional reaction to *Temptation* is not only understandable, but predictable. If a major motion picture studio released a film inaccurately depicting my best friend or a loved and respected relative as an immoral, unbalanced, self–centered fanatic, I would have a distinctly emotional reaction. The average man on the street certainly wouldn't care as much or be hurt as deeply by such a film, simply because he or she doesn't share the relationship that generates the emotion. A film critic might chide me for a lack of artistic perspective. "You don't understand. Portraying your mother as a kleptomaniac makes her more accessible and understandable to others. You can't view this as factual, but as an artistic expression." But I would be compelled to respond, "No. *You* don't understand. My mother is not a kleptomaniac, and I am grossly offended at seeing her character distorted in the name of 'art.'"

In this light, *Temptation* may be far more than a movie. It may very well be a spiritual barometer. If we couldn't "care less" about an overt, distortion–ridden, frontal assault on the character, relationships, and actions of

Christ, perhaps we would "care less" about Christ Himself.

The Response of Integrity

It is clear that when we encounter the person of Jesus Christ there are a number of responses open to us. We can try to take Him down a few pegs by imagining Him as a self–styled junior messiah. We can assign him a place on the dusty back shelf of our lives and promise to think about spiritual things "sometime later when we have a little more time." (This nebulous commitment is usually fulfilled in a deeply introspective minute in front of the TV—preferably during the commercial break between "Wheel of Fortune" and "Jeopardy.") But Jesus is patient and insistent. He continues to make Himself known in our lives, waiting for our response.

How should we respond to Jesus? It's an age–old question that continues to haunt us today. Matthew provides us with an eyewitness account of the first time this watershed issue came to the forefront. "Now when Jesus came to the district of Caesarea Philippi, He began asking His disciples, saying, 'Who do people say that the Son of Man is?' And they said, 'Some say John the Baptist; and others Elijah; but still others, Jeremiah, or one of the prophets'" (Matt. 16:13–14).

The disciples were more than happy to chip in their two cents worth on the controversial issue of the true identity of Christ. Since George Gallup and *The USA Today* wouldn't even exist for another nineteen hundred years, who was more qualified to provide a little marketing input? These men were able to stand around in the crowd while the Master taught or healed or performed miracles. "No problem Jesus. We'll tell you exactly what the man on the street thinks about You. Some take a look at Your incredible miracles and figure You've got to be someone supernatural—like John the Baptist risen from the dead. Others think that with all this talk of the Kingdom of God, maybe You're Elijah, getting everything ready for the end of the world. Still others hear You preaching and it is heavy stuff; that Sermon on the Mount for instance. Convicting... real convicting, kind of like something from Jeremiah or one of the prophets."

"He said to them, 'But who do you say that I am?'

"And Simon Peter answered and said, 'Thou art the Christ, the Son of the Living God'" (Matt. 16:15–16). On a road through the cool high country of northern Palestine, the most significant question ever uttered was asked and answered. A simple fisherman named Simon had looked hard at the life and teaching of Jesus of Nazareth and had come to a life–changing conclusion. This man from Galilee was more than sage, more than prophet, more than a fine moral example. Jesus was God. "And Jesus answered and said to him, 'Blessed are you, Simon Barjona, because flesh and blood did not reveal this to you, but My Father who is in heaven'" (Matt. 16:17).

Simon had found the answer, and his experience points to another inescapably relevant question. When it is our turn to make up our minds about this Jesus, will we rely on fact or fantasy? Will we trust the illusions of Hollywood or the illumination of God's Spirit? Will our answer be based on solid information from the historically reliable witness of the New Testament or the subjective ignorance of the lost and confused?

He asked them, "But who do You say that I am?"

He asks us the same question today.

Discussion Questions

1. Read John 1:1–18. What difference do you see between to Bible's view of Jesus and how He is represented in the media?

2. Does it surprise you that Christians take media portrayals of Jesus so personally? Do you think this is an over reaction? Why or why not?

3. Do you believe the Gospel accounts give an accurate portrait of Jesus? Why or why not?

4. If Jesus were to ask you, "Who do you say that I am?" How would you respond? Explain your answer.

Chapter IX
The Stained Glass Messiah

I can more easily see Jesus Christ sweeping the streets of London than issuing edicts from its cathedrals.

— G. K. Chesterton —

FIRST CAME the westerns. "Gunsmoke," "Bonanza," and "Rawhide" captured the airwaves. As time passed, the sit–coms began asserting their strength in the ratings wars, and America became familiar with zany families from the Clampetts to the Cleavers. From our safe vantage point (hunched over a turkey and mashed potato TV dinner in our dimly lit living rooms), we've watched a seemingly endless and ever–changing parade of network programming pass down the electronic equivalent of Main Street U.S.A.. A type of show will debut, grab the public attention, be subtly and not so subtly copied, become too familiar, and pass away into the media afterlife of cable and syndication.

The programming hit, currently enjoying its moment in the sun, is the live audience TV talk show. This phenomenon began innocently enough. Phil Donahue stretched his wireless mike to the sky and asked a question heavy on the mind of the breathless, swarming, daytime viewing public ("Is the caller there?"). But Phil would not be alone for long. Other personalities would fill other studios with equally caring audiences, prowling the aisles in search of the true heartbeat of trendy America. Oprah Winfrey, Sally Jesse Rafael, and even Geraldo, would take their place alongside the Veg–o–matic and Bugs Bunny as household names.

In order to stay competitive in the cutthroat world of the ratings game, these programs have entered an arms race of sorts. To hold the attention and channel changers of an often jaded and fickle public, a *"National Enquirer* of the Air"* approach is in full bloom. Consider some representative samples of recent in–studio guests: "People married to split personalities," "Victims of UFO kidnappings," even a husband and wife who had sex change operations and remarried each other have offered us their dubious company via the tube. Geraldo has bared it all in an up–close and personal show from a nudist colony, while not to be outdone, Sally Jesse Rafael dressed up as a prostitute and was propositioned on New York's 42nd Street.

The Ultimate Interview

Despite the commitment of these shows to truth, justice, and sensationalism, I'm afraid that Phil, Sally, Oprah, Geraldo, and Mort have been outdone. Andrew Hodges, an Alabama psychiatrist, claims to have conducted an interview with the one guest that would guarantee any of these shows boffo ratings on prime time network television.

Jesus Christ.

Kate DeSmet, writing for the Gannett News Service, reported that Hodges came up with an idea to sit Jesus down—figuratively speaking—and ask Him about everything from the virgin birth to the betrayal by His friend Judas. Whenever details were scarce, Hodges would fill in the gaps with creative writing. "I started looking at the Scriptures the way a psychiatrist looks at the context of a person's life. There was a whole hidden world there which revealed information about the human development of Jesus Christ." A controversial example of this "hidden world" appears when Hodges has Jesus recall getting into a fistfight. At age eleven, some neighborhood bullies taunt Jesus about being born illegitimately. Says Jesus: "When Joseph saw Me, he just looked at My bruises and the cut beneath My eye and said, 'Who won?' I told him, 'I did.' All he said was, 'Good!' My heavenly Father would one day ask Me not to defend Myself in a fight, but until that fight came, He never told Me I couldn't stand up for Myself."[29]

Few would dispute that this is a very "human" story with a nice enough moral, but there remains one small problem with this anecdote. The New Testament never even implies that such a fist fight took place. Hodges responds, "That passage about the fist fight bothers some people. But if you consider the context of His life, it is the sort of thing that could very well have happened."

Hodges' "interview" generates a number of mixed reactions. First, it is this kind of "creative writing" that led to the overblown monstrosity of *The Last Temptation of Christ.* Taking a look at the human side of Christ is one thing, but lowering Him into the depths of sin and violence to make Him more "relatable" is quite another. Like any other historical figure, we do a definite disservice when we distort the facts to conform even an admired individual to our particular taste, mind set, or psychological theory.

Yet even this fanciful account pulls at our heart strings a bit. Growing up in a nominally Christian home, my exposure to the person of Christ was brief and fleeting, usually reserved for the once a year pilgrimage to a main line denominational church for an Easter or Christmas service. Since the person and work of Jesus wasn't discussed in any meaningful way, most of my conception of Christ came from the renaissance–style stained glass renderings that caught my eye. As I fidgeted with my junior–sized bow tie and tried to get comfortable on the hard, wooden pews, I had plenty of time for some amateur theologizing. Who was this Jesus anyway? From all I could gather, He was a blue–eyed, blonde–haired Swede. He clearly needed a haircut, or maybe He was one of those hippies that Dad always laughed at when we drove through San Francisco on vacation. Since He was so skinny, I concluded that His mom hadn't been making Him eat right. A little exercise wouldn't have hurt the guy either. And that halo! How in the world did He manage to keep such a funny hat on His head? It would be murder on a windy day. Add to this His portrayal in the Cecil B. DeMille costume epics we dutifully watched that time of year, and my picture of Christ was complete.

Jesus was a cold, distant, emaciated, northern European mystic who talked like an extra from a local Shakespearean festival. Hardly an attractive or easy to relate to personality by any stretch of the imagination.

Can You Relate?

The current wave of effort to "humanize" Jesus seems to indicate that I was not alone in my early Christian "education." The work of Andrew Hodges (and Martin Scorsese for that matter) can be viewed as a reaction against this aloof and unreal cultural Jesus. It is almost as if, deep inside, we know that there must be more to Him than an ethereal caricature on the ceiling of the Sistine Chapel.

Is Jesus Christ more than simply a stained glass messiah? There is a way to answer this crucial question without having to resort to wild speculation, "creative writing," or trance channeling. In our free–thinking culture we seem content to let each person blithely imagine what Jesus was like, but the eyewitness biographies of the New Testament present a radically different idea. Jesus was and is a real person. He lived in history and He lives today. You and I can discover who He is and what He is like by examining the reliable record of His life and teaching contained in the pages of the New Testament.

Let's get truly personal with Jesus Christ. Let's take an up–close look at an extraordinary incident that reveals significant insights into what made Jesus tick. In the next few pages we'll discover how Jesus related to people, His intense passion over principle, and the awesome power that carved His words indelibly into the very fabric of human history. Rather than trusting in the subjective, or even the traditional, let's go to the source and get acquainted with the Jesus of the Bible.

Christ and People

It doesn't take a Ph.D. in psychology to come to the conclusion that human beings are extremely social creatures. Relationships are of such supreme value to us that with them we grow and thrive, without them we wither and die. The value of personal interaction is constantly underscored in our culture. From the pages of classic literature to the images of corny tearjerker movies on the late–late show, it is clear that the ultimate measure of a man or woman is not accomplishment, achievement, or amassed wealth, but the quality of an individual's personal relationships.

Interestingly, we can evaluate the life of Jesus Christ using this same standard. How did Jesus relate to people? What sort of impact did He make on the lives of those who interacted with Him? We gain real insight into Jesus' relational style in this account of a group of desperate men making a desperate move.

> *And when He had come back to Capernaum several days afterward, it was heard that He was at home. And many were gathered together, so that there was no longer room, even near the door; and He was speaking the word to them. And they came, bringing to Him a paralytic, carried by four men. And being unable to get to Him because of the crowd, they removed the roof above Him; and when they had dug an opening, they let down the*

pallet on which the paralytic was lying"
(Mark 2:14).

Mark paints a vivid word picture of what was going on in this sleepy lakeside village. A huge crowd had massed together, thronging to see this miracle–working prophet, finally back in His own home town. Talk was that perhaps this Jesus was more than a prophet. Could He be the promised Messiah? Could this visit be prophecy fleshing out before our very eyes? In the parlance of show biz, Jesus was doing great box office. He was definitely the hottest ticket in town.

His own home had been overwhelmed by this sudden wave of popularity and curiosity. This once humble dwelling was now bursting at the seams with local dignitaries and common folk, all intent on getting a chance to size up Christ for themselves. It was hot. It was crowded. It was a standing–room–only situation.

On the outside looking in were five men with a compelling mission and a confounding problem. One of them was paralyzed and helpless. The other four were carrying him on a crude wooden pallet. Jesus had done tremendous miracles in the surrounding countryside. As they sized up the huge throng of people in front of them, two questions raced through their minds. Could His touch be enough to heal even this seemingly hopeless condition? And even if Jesus had the power to help, how in the world could they get close to Him in a mob scene like this?

Suddenly, it hit them. It was a bold, even an outrageous idea; the kind of plan that draws blank stares and hesitations but usually passes when someone asks, "Well, does anyone have a better suggestion?" The silence and shrugs made it unanimous. They would climb up on the roof, take a good guess as to where Jesus was, and start digging. First the sunbaked clay and tiles began to crumble and give way. Then the wood and palm thatching became visible. Inside, some members of Jesus' audience began to shoot irritated glances at the ceiling as small, falling fragments began to interrupt their concentration.

Soon, an impromptu skylight began to take shape. The hole became larger and larger until finally the space was judged wide enough. With some hastily borrowed ropes, the crude stretcher was lowered. A paralyzed and desperate man found himself slowly swinging in front of Jesus and a shocked and silent crowd.

No doubt the emotional atmosphere in that room was thick and conflicting. The religious experts in attendance were miffed that this group of men would be forceful and ill–mannered enough to interrupt their discussion with such an entrance. The owner of the house was none too thrilled at the prospect of the impromptu interior design renovation taking place above his head.

And then there was the paralytic. How would you have felt lying on his pallet? This man was caught in an emotional grinder. Undoubtedly he was embarrassed to be thrust to the forefront of such a packed and impatient crowd, yet relieved that his friends' crazy scheme had worked. Hopeless and desperate, it is possible that the tyranny of his condition had never seemed so sharply unbearable as at this moment, yet as he made eye contact with the Teacher, the soft, almost inaudible sound of hope persistently whispered, "But what if… ?"

In this chaotic, tension–charged moment Jesus slowly moved toward the paralytic. He glanced upward at the four intent faces peering down through the hole in the roof. "And seeing their faith, He said, 'Friend, your sins are forgiven you'" (Luke 5:20).

At first blush the tenderness of Christ is quite apparent in this encounter. Jesus didn't maintain an aloof, uncaring, mannequin–like posture in this situation. Breaking the tension of self–consciousness and uncertainty, Christ leaned over, and touched this helpless man.

Come Again, Jesus?

The words Christ chose, even though spoken in deep compassion, leave many confused. Here we have a paralytic, making a desperate bid to be healed. Through a radical and daring plan he makes it to the Master, only to hear Him say, "Friend, Your sins are forgiven you."

Don't tell me; you're thinking it too. "Great, Jesus. We know that You put great stock in the spiritual, but I think You've missed the point. This guy didn't come for confession or counseling. He came for a miracle. Forgiveness is nice, but this isn't the time or place." Some even liken Jesus' approach to finding a dehydrated man in the desert and saying, "Sorry, I don't have any water for you. But you're looking a tad over–exposed. How about a little sunscreen?"

Anatomy of a Conflict

This very popular line of reasoning illustrates one of the greatest points of conflict between God and man through the centuries. We as human beings have to live on planet Earth. Day–to–day life for us is often one long struggle with physical needs and concerns. If we don't sleep, we get physically tired. If we don't eat, we get physically hungry. If we don't work, we get physically cold when the electric company shuts off the power to our Toastmaster 5000 Space Heater and Waffle Iron. This painfully obvious and persistent chain of cause–and–effect presents such a strong and demanding presence in our lives that we come to believe in a distorted worldview that insists that the physical is all that really matters. "After all," the cynical observe, "you can't eat an ideal. You can't warm yourself by wrapping a commitment around your frozen toes. You can't expect a belief to keep the rain off your back."

If you want to grab the attention of man, deal with the physical. Scripture provides an example of this truth in the public ministry of Christ. Jesus' popularity hit its high–watermark, not when He preached the Sermon on the

Mount or walked on water, but when He fed a crowd, numbering at least five thousand, with a few small loaves of bread and a couple of fish. This fed and satisfied crowd had been won over. They would have followed Jesus anywhere. But surprisingly, Jesus withdrew from them. His explanation was startling. "Truly, truly, I say to you, you seek Me, not because you saw signs, but because you ate of the loaves, and were filled. Do not work for the food which perishes, but for the food which endures to eternal life, which the Son of Man will give to you, for on Him the Father, even God, has set His seal" (John 6:26–27).

Man and God have a conflicting set of priorities. Man looks at the world and declares, "The spiritual is important, but the physical really matters." God looks at the world and says, "The physical is important, but the spiritual really matters." Sounds like the stuff of an endless debate, doesn't it? But this age–old battle of perspective resolves itself when we add a real factor to our discussion—the passage of time. Because time passes and man ages, the person who devotes his life to meeting his physical needs is fighting a losing battle. Sooner or later, no matter how adept we are at earning a living, keeping in shape, or amassing wealth, age robs us of our ability to keep up the pace. Inescapably we are all faced with the ultimate physical reality—death. That notion terrifies those whose eggs are all in the physical basket. We occasionally read of celebrities who sleep in decompression chambers hoping to prolong life, or people who are frozen in hopes that science will someday cure their illnesses (not to mention come up with a way to thaw out a human popsicle), but at best we delay the inevitable. No matter how well–fed, clothed, and pampered, the human body eventually runs out of steam and expires.

From this perspective, the condition of our souls takes on a heightened sense of importance. The long and winding road of life leads us all to our ultimate day in court. An actual day and time yet in the future called "Judgment

Day." In simple and unmistakable terms, the Bible summarizes our common destiny: "It is appointed for men to die once and after this comes judgment." (Heb. 9:27)

In the words of an old German proverb, "Forever is a long bargain." If you could have the choice of sixty, seventy, eighty years on this planet, with every physical need met, or assurance that your sins would be forgiven on judgment day, which would you take? From God's perspective, a point of view that takes in all eternity, the choice is academic.

"Friend, your sins are forgiven you." Jesus was meeting this physically and spiritually paralyzed man's needs inside out. He loved people too much to put a physical band–aid on a spiritual tumor. Jesus refused to meet a temporal need without also dealing with the heart.

Christ and Principle

Back in that dusty, overcrowded, Capernaum living room, an incredibly tender moment takes place. Before a stunned and silent crowd, Jesus is face–to–face with a hopeless and hurting man on a pallet.

"Take courage, my son. Your sins are forgiven." At the very core of his being, years of guilt and recrimination, both deserved and undeserved, were being lifted away. A mob scene had been transformed into a quiet moment of reconciliation between God and man.

But as the old saying goes, you can't please everybody. "But there were some of the scribes sitting there and reasoning in their hearts, 'Why does this man speak that way? He is blaspheming; who can forgive sins but God alone?'" (Mark 2:6–7).

The words of Christ, so direct and encouraging to the paralytic, had a distinctly different effect on the religious leaders who watched from an uninvolved distance. This simple statement, "Your sins are forgiven," had slammed like a wrecking ball into the superstructure of their concrete reinforced theological sensibilities. Sure, it was well within the boundaries of propriety for a prophet to heal, but to forgive sin? That was a different matter entirely.

The Right to Forgive

The reasoning of these leaders wasn't off–base. Forgiveness, after all, is the sole prerogative of the offended party. If you and I were riding on a bus together, and for no reason at all I smacked you in the face, you would have good reason to be a bit put out at my behavior. But how would you react if the person sitting next to you turned to me and said, "Don't worry about that person's bloody nose. I forgive you for belting him"? Undoubtedly you would be in a state of anger and disbelief, or perhaps find yourself looking around for Alan Funt, convinced that this was some bizarre version of "Candid Camera Meets Rambo." You could easily find yourself almost as angry at this offerer of clemency as at me, yelling, "Who are you to let this guy off the hook? I'm the one with the broken nose!" Common sense tells us that only the directly wronged can grant forgiveness.

These scribes knew their Old Testament, and they knew a thing or two about sin. No sooner had Jesus finished His sentence than the words of King David came to their racing minds. "Against Thee, Thee only, I have sinned, And done what is evil in Thy sight, So that Thou art justified when Thou dost speak, And blameless when Thou dost judge" (Ps. 51:4).

When we think of those wronged by the evil in this world, our focus is limited to the perspective of people. After all, how is God affected when someone's purse is snatched or a stockbroker tosses ethics out the window to make some extra cash? The surprising truth is that God Himself is directly wronged by every immoral act of humanity. God is not some disinterested third party minding His part of the universe while we mind ours. God created us for a reason. Not to claw our way to the top of some evolutionary dog pile, but to be direct recipients of His goodness and love, to bear His image, and to share that goodness with others. When we, by an act of our own will, decide to reject that goodness and love in favor of selfishness and hate, we do far more than simply make this world a tougher place to live in—we break faith with God. In essence we stand before our Creator and say, "Sure You said, 'Thou shalt not steal,' 'Thou shalt not lie,' 'Thou shalt not commit adultery,' but what do You know any way? Pack up Your commandments and standards and take a hike!"

These religious experts well understood that God is the ultimate offended party in all human sin. It was up to the Judge of all humanity to declare guilt or innocence, punishment or forgiveness. And if this is the case, who was Jesus to make such an outrageously presumptuous pronouncement? Who did He think He was?

Their reasoning was on target; only God can forgive sin. Their alternatives were clear and unmistakable. They either had to get down on their knees and worship Jesus or accuse Him of blasphemy, and blasphemy was a capital offense in those days.

So, What's on Your Mind?

The theological debate that was raging in the minds of these scribes didn't escape the notice of Jesus. One of the most difficult aspects of trying to deal with a person like Christ was noted by the apostle John: "But Jesus, on His part, was not entrusting Himself to them, for He knew all men, and because He did not need anyone to bear witness concerning man for He Himself knew what was in man" (John 2:2–25).

Can you imagine what it would have been like to interact with a person who knew your every thought, your every word, even before you spoke? The closest to this set of circumstances I have ever been was when I was around four years old. Dinner traditionally was served around

6:00 P.M., but my appetite would invariably start warming up around 5:00 P.M. This condition obviously called for every four–year–old's idea of a balanced meal—just enough cookies to balance in both hands. Standing in the way of meeting my basic physical needs at this point were two formidable obstacles. First, I would have to slink into the kitchen and climb up what seemed to be a ten–foot–high counter to get my hands on that smiling, bear–shaped treasure trove of sweets, the cookie jar. Second, I would have to accomplish this mission without tipping off my mom that her second son's healthy appetite was about to be buried under a pile of chocolate cookies and that wonderful white stuff they squeezed in between. Every now and again I managed to pull off my junior version of Mission: Impossible. With a stealth befitting a jewel thief, I was able to silently climb up the counter, grab the goods, and make a clean get–away. With a few hurried chomps, the last traces of physical evidence were hidden away in my slightly over–satisfied stomach. The perfect crime had been committed.

Then, as I straightened my halo, my mom would walk back into the kitchen. She would take one look at me, standing there with the most innocent smile you ever saw on my face, and she'd start to frown. "What did I tell you about eating Oreos this close to dinner?"

The wheels of justice turned quickly. I was sentenced to a mandatory ten to fifteen (minutes) in solitary (the go–to–your–room routine). As I trudged down the hall to lock–up, my mind would be reeling. "I was perfect, just perfect. No noise. No stepping on the cat. No broken cookie jar. What gave me away? How did she nail me again?" Was it some maternal sixth sense? Or could it have been this attractive black–Oreo–fragment Fu Man Chu mustache that graced my four–year–old face?

How did Jesus know the reasoning of these men's hearts? It could have been a roll of the eye, a look of shock or disgust that betrayed them. It may have been a clear example of a variation on the old saw: "You can fool some of the people some of the time, but don't try to put one over on God."

Jesus knew their thoughts. He turned away from the paralytic and asked a simple, but startling question. "Why are you reasoning about these things in your hearts? Which is easier, to say to the paralytic, 'Your sins are forgiven'; or to say, 'Arise, and take up your pallet and walk'?" (Mark 2:8–9).

The Exasperating Jesus

Do you catch what just happened? In the span of less than a minute, Jesus has transformed a moment of tender compassion with the handicapped to sharp confrontation with the hard–hearted. From a human standpoint, it's easy to find ourselves getting exasperated with Christ. We want to pull Him aside and say, "Look, why don't you leave well enough alone and ignore these clowns? The paralytic understands what You've said. Why not just settle for that? You can't please everybody. No one gets 100 percent support anyway."

Why does Jesus raise this confrontive issue? Because He well understood the value of truth. He knew that peace at the expense of truth is no peace at all.

Truth Behind the Mike

This point was driven home to me on a phone in religious talk show. The topic of debate was the nature of salvation: What must we do to inherit eternal life? As you can guess there were some serious differences of opinion flying around the studio that night. The host of the program asked the rabbi on the panel, "From your stand–point, what must a Gentile do to be saved?" The rabbi replied that if a non–Jewish person lived a good life and took care of his family, that God would accept him. It was a nice, warm sentiment. The rest of the panel was smiling and nodding. It was at that moment I made my crucial mistake. I winced.

The host picked up on my reaction like a shot.

"Well, Pastor Richards, I see that you take exception to that point of view." (The tone of his voice made it sound like I disagreed with baseball, Mother's Day, and saving ice–trapped whales.)

I replied, "Please don't misunderstand me. What the rabbi says is a wonderful sentiment. I only wish it were true. The problem is his statement is completely subjective."

The rabbi, visibly irritated by my remark, shot back, "What do you mean, 'subjective'?"

"Rabbi, you and I agree on one point. We both believe that the first five books of the Bible, the books of Moses, are divinely inspired, the very word of God. Is that a fair statement?"

"Well, yes. But I don't see...."

"Rabbi, if you can show me one verse from the books of Moses that substantiates your claim that Gentiles will make it to heaven by being good enough, I'll believe it."

There was a long and pregnant pause, then the host jumped in and changed the subject.

Who won the argument? It really didn't matter. Suffice it to say an interfaith friendship wasn't born that night. I used to leave that studio with my stomach doing a rumba version of "Flight of the Bumblebee." Why? Because I hate conflict. Those who know me will tell you I would rather play barefooted hopscotch in a room full of thumbtacks than cause an argument. But clearly, some things are worth the price of disagreement.

Jesus understood that principle. He forced a simple question with staggering implications to the forefront.

"Which is easier for God, to forgive sins or heal a paralyzed man with a simple command?"

Christ and Power

Jesus Christ was a person of incredible balance and depth. In this one instance we see Him dealing with people with a heart of tender compassion, while not sacrificing rock–hard integrity and conviction. As Sir Norman Anderson once observed:

> *One of the most remarkable things about Him was the perfect balance of character He displayed. It is a truism that a man's strong points nearly always carry with them corresponding weaknesses. He may be an extrovert or an introvert; he may be sanguine or melancholic, choleric or phlegmatic; or he may in some degree combine two or three of these temperaments. But he never succeeds in achieving a perfect balance—a sympathy which is never weak, a strength which is never insensitive, a benevolence which is never indulgent, or a drive which is never ruthless. Jesus, alone, seems to have achieved this balance; and in Him every temperament finds both its ideal and its correction. He was a man, not a woman, yet women as much as men find their perfect example in Him. He was a Jew, not a European, African, or Indian; yet men and women of every race find in Him all they would most wish to be.*[30]

Jesus' force of personality certainly had an impact on those around Him, but what made Christ truly outstanding came next. "'But in order that you may know that the Son of Man has authority on earth to forgive sins'—He said to the paralytic—'I say to you, rise, take up your pallet and go home.' And he rose immediately took up the pallet and went out in the sight of all; so that they were all amazed and were glorifying God, saying, 'We have never seen anything like this'" (Mark 2:10–12).

In perfect control and dignity, Jesus turns back to this helpless man lying on a crude wooden stretcher. He spoke a simple, even understated command, "Rise. Take up your pallet and go home." No jumping. No screaming. No shaking of the person in need. No appeals for money.

Imagine this incident from the paralytic's point of view. First, a sense of shock, confusion, even disbelief. "Rise? Take my pallet and go home? How am I supposed to rise when my limp and atrophied body won't obey? Thanks for nothing..."

But then a startling sensation. Like a switch had been thrown or a fuse replaced, long dormant circuits of nerves fired back to life. The brain, unaccustomed to the common impulses we take for granted, was suddenly deluged with a flood of feeling. More striking, a sense of movement. Strands of muscle tissue, long out of commission, came back on line, wonderfully obedient again.

First one foot, then two on the floor. He soaked up every nuance. The texture, even the temperature of the ground was a sensual feast. Then, for the first time in pain–racked, frustration–ridden, hopeless weeks, his shoulder and back muscles flexed. Knees locked. He rose. His friends, peering through the roof in stunned silence, aghast. "We hoped, but who could have really expected...?"

What else does a person do at that point, but obey? He took up the pallet and went home. And what a homecoming it undoubtedly was.

The Meaning of a Miracle

Why did Jesus perform this unprecedented act? Some suggest compassion for the hurting, and certainly that was part of His motivation. But even more importantly Jesus was proving a point. Remember the $64,000 theological question of the day—"Who can forgive sins but God alone?" True forgiveness is the most precious gift that any person can ever receive, but it does have one flaw. For all its profound eternal implications, forgiveness is invisible. We can't distill it, can it, or weigh it on the scales. We can observe the difference forgiveness makes in a life over time, but who in that room had the patience to wait and see?

So Jesus forced the issue. He did the impossible, and the people didn't miss the significance of what had taken place. Their reaction was not one of smug, semi–conscious, stained glass bliss. Luke tells us they were "...seized with astonishment" and "...filled with fear, saying, 'We have seen remarkable things today.'"

This reaction to a clear demonstration of God's power underscores an important point. Miracles were not simply magic tricks, foisted on a gullible, unsophisticated, pre–scientific people. If we could transfer the same set of circumstances to the intensive care unit of a modern research hospital the reactions would be no different. The natural order of things dictates that paralyzed people do not simply get up, pick up their pallets, and walk home. But the natural order of things was interfered with as a miracle occurred.

So why did Jesus heal this man? To wow a crowd? No. To relieve suffering? Partially.

But more importantly, Jesus knew that actions speak louder than words. It was one thing to declare a man's sins were forgiven, quite another to prove it. The outward miracle of healing a person of a most desperate physical problem showed the greater, inward healing of man's most desperate spiritual problem. Which was easier, to forgive sin or heal the paralyzed with a word?

For God, both are equally possible.

Don't miss the message. In that small room, in a small house in Capernaum, an obscure, dusty, lake–side town, stood no less than God in human flesh. Jesus had presented His divine credentials.

From Religion to Reality

It is clear that many people today are becoming increasingly dissatisfied with religion once–removed from reality. Some are attempting to clear away the cobwebs of formalism and tradition to take a fresh look at who God is and what He is saying to us. At this point a fair question is raised. If we are going to understand the real Jesus, why focus on this particular incident? What can a day in the life of a paralyzed man and some impromptu living room remodeling teach us about ultimate reality?

Simply put, this account tells us some crucial things about Jesus that we will never hear on Geraldo or see in stained glass. In His compassion, in His willingness to involve Himself, to touch the lives of those around Him, it is evident that Jesus was no ethereal, aloof, other–worldly mystic. His warmth and accessibility stand in sharp distinction to the examples of contemporary "holy men."

God in a Limo?

One of the most pathetic sights captured on film in the '80s was the daily, afternoon devotional hour at a place called Rajneeshpuram, Oregon. Ardent, red–clad disciples would gather along the main street of their sixty–four–thousand–acre commune waiting for the spiritual highlight of their well–regimented day. A man they considered to be no less than God, the Bhagwan Shree Rajneesh, would commune with his followers by driving by them in a chauffeured Rolls Royce. Even though contact with their master consisted of nothing more than an impassive wave from a half–rolled–down car window, the devotees would excitedly share the incredible depth of love they felt from this "ascended teacher." In marked contrast, Jesus never left His expression of love to the imagination. Jesus cared. Jesus touched. Jesus healed.

A Passion for the Truth

The second characteristic of Christ we can glean from this encounter in Capernaum is His passion for the truth.

When the religious leaders in the gathering were inwardly outraged at His declaration that the paralytic's sins were forgiven him, Jesus could have easily preserved the peace. If He had bought into the giddy pluralism of our day He could have conveniently said, "Well, I see that your very sincere religious sensibilities have been offended. I'm sorry. Some people will accept Me as God and some won't. Believe whatever you like. Far be it for Me to insist that you all see things My way." But there is no mistaking the fact that Jesus held to a precise view of ultimate reality. He wouldn't let wrong conclusions about Himself slide on by. When eternity is on the line, truth matters, and that can be a threatening concept these days. As Ted Koppel commented in his commencement address at Duke University: "Our society finds truth too strong a medicine to digest undiluted. In its purest form, truth is not a polite tap on the shoulder; it is a howling reproach. What Moses brought down from Mount Sinai were not the Ten Suggestions, they are the Ten Commandments."

This flies in the face of the shotgun approach to spirituality so evident today. Some groups look at Jesus and label Him a good teacher. Others say He was the archangel Michael; some say He was Satan's spirit brother. Still others see Him as a product of fast-forward evolution or even a UFO being. The general consensus is "Buy into whatever picture of Christ you like, as long as it works for you." But in this brief dramatic incident, Jesus leaves no doubt as to Who He truly is. He didn't leave His deity as a point open for discussion. As C. S. Lewis put it:

> "I'm ready to accept Jesus as a great moral teacher, but I don't accept His claim to be God." That is the one thing we must not say. A man who was merely a man and said the sort of things Jesus said would not be a great moral teacher. He would either be a lunatic— on a level with the man who says he is a poached egg—or else He would be the Devil of Hell. You must make your choice. Either this man was, and is, the Son of God; or else a

madman or something worse. You can shut Him up for a fool, you can spit at Him and kill Him as a demon, or you can fall at His feet and call Him Lord and God.

But let us not come with any patronizing nonsense about His being a great human teacher. He has not left that open to us.

He did not intend to.[31]

It was the realization that there was much more to Jesus Christ than Renaissance art could ever capture that changed my life. Tradition cannot hem Jesus in; the fog of popular opinion cannot obscure Him for long. Our endless religious squabbling cannot drown out His clear call, but for many, a stained glass messiah is all they want. After all, it's much easier to deal with Jesus the museum piece than Jesus the messiah. A picture of Jesus will hang dutifully on a wall, silent and inert. The Person of Jesus has the annoying habit of coming to our well–ordered lives and asking tough questions. "Where are you going? What are you doing with the life that I have given you? Are you ready to face your ultimate destination? Do you really know Me after all?"

You see, the stained glass messiah, like a lot of other things in this life, is a distraction. It cleverly keeps us from coming to grips with the real item, from truly hearing His call to our souls. But the distraction doesn't make Jesus any less real. The real Jesus still comes to our lives with a compelling invitation. "Behold, I stand at the door and knock; if anyone hears My voice and opens the door, I will come in to him, and will dine with him, and he with Me" (Rev. 3:20).

When He knocks will you hear?

When He knocks will you answer?

Discussion   Questions

1. Read John 13:1–11. What insights into Jesus' personality do you see in this passage?

2. If Jesus were physically present here today, where do you think we would find Him? What would He be doing?

3. If you were face to face with Jesus, would you find the idea that He knows everything about you comforting or challenging? Explain your answer.

Chapter X
Now Bring Out
the Figgy Pudding

He who has not Christmas in his heart will never find it under a tree.

— Roy L. Smith —

A LONG time ago (before the advent of cable television or even home computers), in a place far, far away called Oxnard, California, stood a small kindergarten–through–eighth–grade school called Mesa Union.

Every year when Christmas time would roll around, certain regular and predictable events began to take place in our world, especially once we reached junior high. Early December meant that the precious hours for after–school skate board competitions and vacant lot football games were cut to a bare minimum as dusk came earlier and earlier, falling over our quiet valley like a wool blanket. The impending arrival of winter was heavy in the air as the first signs of morning frost became noticeable. Nights were filled with the sounds of wind machines and the smell of smoldering smudge pots as local ranchers began their yearly battle to preserve their citrus crops.

December was a wonderful time. It not only brought the stuff that Garrison Keillor–esque memories are made of— the warm, the calm, the familiar—the end of the year also ushered in a fair share of excitement and variety to our lives as well. The well–worn pattern of junior high routine would take a few weeks off as we reveled in serious deviations from the all–too–predictable norm. After trudging through a dull and lifeless November, December would bring:

- The traditional Mesa Union Junior High Christmas Party. This crudely festive event gave us the opportunity to wolf down enough sugar cookies and red–death punch to put our adolescent nervous systems in orbit for a week. Unfortunately the party was inevitably cut short when the classmate voted "Most Likely to Do Five to Ten in San Quentin" was caught throwing a Hostess Ding Dong snack cake at some unsuspecting victim across the room.
- The glorious prospect of two weeks away from school work. Christmas vacation brought welcome relief from the intense pleasure of studying the industrial revolution, peering helplessly at algebra problems, and trying desperately to remember where to stick participles when diagramming sentences.
- And, of course, the unbridled spectacle and pageantry of the annual Mesa Union Christmas play.

Ah, yes, the Mesa Union Christmas play. Preparations for this annual event were a highlight of the academic year. For three fun–filled weeks we not only got an hour away from school work for rehearsals, we also enjoyed the bonus of watching our social studies teacher go through the various stages of a nervous breakdown. Let's face it, trying to get a bunch of unruly, sugar–and–hormone–crazed junior high students to learn songs and recite lines in King James English should qualify a person for the Nobel Prize, sainthood, or (at the very least) early retirement.

Not that this adventure in stage production left us completely cold and uninterested. There were two roles in the pageant that grabbed our attention because of their traditional high status. The most popular girl in the eighth grade was always selected to play the role of the Virgin

Mary. This demanding theatrical exercise largely consisted of kneeling next to a makeshift wooden cradle while staring adoringly at the light bulb designed to simulate the baby Jesus. Although some who performed the part complained of blue spots in front of their eyes, the role of Mary, which had no lines, was hardly what's known in show biz parlance as a "stretch."

There was also no question which part was most coveted by the guys. Every year this holiday play would begin with a very predictable scene. The most popular eighth–grade boy would walk out on stage in a Roman soldier's suit, open a scroll, and announce that "All the world must be taxed. Let everyone return to their place of birth to be counted."

A brief moment on stage? A bit part? To be sure. But from a junior high point of view, any acting role that allowed a person to carry a sword and wear a nifty bronze breastplate was considered cool, very cool.

And since the Roman soldier and the Virgin Mary inevitably started going steady after the pageant, there was no shortage of fledgling actors vying for the part. When the audition sign–up sheet went around there were invariably thirty–two names scrawled under "Roman soldier." Reading for this step to social stardom was an incredible struggle against nature, as thirty–one of us strained to look larger and more menacing than our thirteen years would allow. If you could have harnessed the energy we expended in trying to keep our squeaky adolescent voices in a basso profundo range (somewhere between Orson Welles and Tennessee Ernie Ford), you could have lit Los Angeles for a week.

Unfortunately for the majority of us, the part always went to some eighth–grader who, through a quirk of genetic fate, was already six feet tall and could actually grow a semblance of a mustache. The rest of us were left to curse our luck and settle for being a shepherd or adding our cracking baritone/sopranos to the Mesa Union Christmas choir.

Every year this cycle would repeat. Since the script for this holiday extravaganza was originally written in 1956, the music and the message of the play were very familiar. The Roman soldier swaggered out on stage. The Virgin Mary stared adoringly at the light bulb. The end of the final performance signaled the start of Christmas vacation. We ran shrieking into the parking lot to celebrate our new–found freedom. A few sensitive parents attempted to comfort the shell–shocked, nerve–frayed director who sat in a corner muttering "Never again... Never, ever again..."

A Holiday Puzzle

From my thirteen–year–old perspective Christmas was a great time of year, but it didn't make a whole lot of sense.

The songs we sang at events like this were warm and traditional, but to my mind a little weird. "Sleep in heavenly peas"? What a disgusting thought. Those awful green appetite–killers looked bad enough on a dinner plate (especially when they were allowed to cool to room temperature as we desperately tried to avoid having to eat them), but sleeping in a bed full of veggies seemed a tiny bit strange.

"God and cinders reconciled"? This was perhaps the most baffling line of all. What did God have to do with a pile of ashes? Well, cinders come from hot places, so I thought, "How nice. Christmas is such a time of peace and good will that even God and the devil bury the hatchet."

I certainly wasn't alone in my cluelessness about Christmas. As we stood in our nicely formed rows, jealously eyeing the Roman soldier and the Virgin Mary, belting out these and other familiar songs, few of us had any idea whatsoever what the words meant. No one ever explained to us what we were singing. It was assumed that we knew what this time of year was all about.

So Close and Yet...

Reality consistently defied that assumption. If you asked the average Mesa Union junior high student about the true meaning of Christmas, we would have replied, "Uh, peace on earth?" (After all that's what the Coke commercials told us.)

"Good will toward men?" (Even the Vietnam war took a day off on Christmas.)

"Baby Jesus, mother Mary and the three wise guys?" (Their plastic likenesses always showed up in the park that time of year.)

As is so often the case, Christmas to us was as much about Good King Wenceslaus and figgy pudding as about anything of eternal, spiritual importance.

Isn't it funny how near to the truth we can be and still flat–out miss it?

During my eighth grade year at Mesa Union, I was given the dubious honor of having a speaking part in the annual Christmas pageant. I refer to this as a dubious honor because it was a classic no–win situation. We all knew very well how the social dynamics of junior high life would come into play in this set of circumstances. Do too well in front of the parents, and you could end up being labeled a goody two–shoes (the rough equivalent of social suicide). Blow your lines completely, and you heard about choking in the clutch for the next six months. As you can well imagine, mediocrity was the order of the day. As in few other situations, being innocuously average was a real accomplishment at the Mesa Union Christmas pageant.

My personal brush with averageness involved standing up and delivering a short paragraph from memory. I call this paragraph "short" only in retrospect. As I gazed at the freshly mimeographed sheet that contained my part, it looked as long as volume "A" of the Encyclopedia

Britannica. How in the world was I ever going to memorize all this?

The fear of going blank on the stage was real enough in my mind that I devoted significant time to memorizing my short soliloquy. I even passed on a prime opportunity to play mud football to make sure I had my assignment down cold. That short collection of words made an indelible mark on my consciousness; in fact, I can still quote them word for word today.

> *And there were in the same country shepherds abiding in the field, keeping watch over their flock by night. And, lo, the angel of the Lord came upon them, and the glory of the Lord shone round about them: and they were sore afraid. And the angel said unto them, Fear not: for, behold, I bring you good tidings of great joy, which shall be to all people. For unto you is born this day in the city of David a Saviour, which is Christ the Lord. And this shall be a sign unto you; Ye shall find the babe wrapped in swaddling clothes, lying in a manger. And suddenly there was with the angel a multitude of the heavenly host praising God and saying, Glory to God in the highest, and on earth peace, good will toward men* (Luke 2:8–14).

As I stood up for my moment of truth, eyes blinded by the spotlight like a rabbit in the headlights of a jeep, I never realized the incredible profundity of the words I was speaking, nor how close to a life–changing realization I was. I simply wanted to reel off my lines and get this source of anxiety over with and out of my life.

It's Beginning to Look a Lot Like...

Ironically, around the holidays being scant inches from the edge of truth is not the sole province of the stage–fright–racked junior higher. The day after Thanksgiving signals the start of the Christmas season in our culture. Christmas tree lots start springing up like weeds in parking lots and open patches of ground across town. Advertising

works itself into a fever pitch as everything from
Christmas champagne to "Teenage Mutant Ninja Turtles"
are pitched to us on the tube. The climate controlled
atmosphere of the local shopping mall overheats under the
strain of thousands of jostling shoppers exchanging
traditional holiday greetings. ("Outta my way or you're
dead meat!") Add to this the pressure of visiting relatives,
over–extended charge cards, and that ominous–looking
pile of five hundred unaddressed Christmas cards that we
swore would be more personalized this year, and "the
season to be jolly" becomes a season less to be enjoyed
than survived.

But buried somewhere underneath the din and demands
of the Yuletide lies a hidden meaning; a meaning that won't
be discovered at half–time of a bowl game or on a Bob
Hope Christmas special. The true meaning of Christmas
can only be discovered by returning to the ancient
beginnings of this event, to the roots of Christianity itself.
To remove the shroud of myth from Christmas we must
grasp the impact of the first Christmas on real people,
ordinary individuals caught up in a most extraordinary
event—the birth of the Son of God.

Christmas and Mary

At one time or another, perhaps in church or in a junior
high Christmas pageant, we've all been exposed to the
basic Christian belief concerning the birth of Jesus Christ.
We know that somehow this whole thing happened in
God's great plan to reach out to a world gone astray. But
what we often fail to realize is that God's plan didn't take
place in a vacuum, or on a chalk board in some theology
school, or in an unknowable higher spiritual realm. The
birth of Jesus Christ took place right here on planet Earth,
with tremendous impact on the lives of people; real,
average, run–of–the–mill people, a lot like you and me.

Consider the overwhelming consequences of the birth of
Jesus Christ on a woman named Mary. Contrary to

popular belief, Mary didn't grow up with a halo glowing over her head. She was an average Jewish young woman, growing up in a below average Jewish town called Nazareth. How could she possibly know that a plan devised before time began was about to collide with her humble life?

> *Now in the sixth month the angel Gabriel was sent from God to a city of Galilee, called Nazareth, to a virgin engaged to a man whose name was Joseph, of the descendants of David; and the virgin's name was Mary... And the angel said to her, "Do not be afraid, Mary; for you have found favor with God. And behold, you will conceive in your womb, and bear a son, and you shall name Him Jesus..." And Mary said to the angel, "How can this be, since I am a virgin?" And the angel answered and said to her, "The Holy Spirit will come upon you, and the power of the Most High will overshadow you; and for that reason the holy offspring shall be called the Son of God... For nothing will be impossible with God"* (Luke 1:26, 27, 30, 31, 34, 35, 37).

When we think of people who are singled out of a huge crowd for an extraordinary turn of events, it's easy to imagine the stunned and dazed filling station attendant in Buckeye, Arizona, who wins three million dollars in the lottery. It must feel strange to think that out of the millions who dump discretionary income into such a hopeless cause every week, *you* were the one who was selected. You are now an overnight millionaire. It really happened to you, and life will never be the same.

If we can hardly grasp being singled out for something that happens every week like winning a lottery, imagine how Mary must have felt receiving this staggering piece of news (delivered by angelic messenger, no less). "Mary, out of the millions of people who have lived and died on earth, God has chosen you to take part in His entrance on the human scene. The Son of God will come into this world by way of your womb."

Now Wait Just a Minute...

It has been said that God's timing is always perfect. The particular time frame, the cultural atmosphere, the very people involved were all carefully selected. It is no mystery to me why Christ was born nearly two thousand years ago and not in our day. Could you imagine how a person living in our semi–rational, "me–first" generation would react to such a unique announcement?

"Sorry, Lord, but from what I understand abstinence is the one foolproof method of birth control. We all know that virgin births are impossible."

"Uh, yeah, that's a great idea Lord, but I really had some other plans for my life over the next few years. Look, call me back and we'll see about scheduling a more convenient time."

"God, think of this from my perspective. Being an unwed mother is not the best way to win friends and influence people. This is not a great career move. Can't we think of some other way?"

Mary, probably all of fifteen years old, had a stunningly different response. "And Mary said, 'Behold the bondslave of the Lord; be it done to me according to your word'" (Luke 1:38).

The term Mary uses to describe herself is significant. At the time of Christ, slavery was a thriving institution, woven almost inextricably into the fabric of Roman–dominated society. Most slaves (as the name implies) served involuntarily. In the days before the advent of Visa, American Express, and convenient monthly payments, if someone ran up some serious debts he or she couldn't pay, the authorities enforced a period of servitude to balance the books. By and large, servitude in Roman slavery was a grueling and humiliating experience, but occasionally an interesting psychological phenomenon took place. Over the years some slaves developed a strong sense of attachment to their owner or the family they served. Some slaves even went so far as to waive their right to freedom and commit themselves to permanent voluntary servitude out of deep sense of love. If this was their choice, they went through a public ceremony and received a new title—bondslave.

How interesting that Mary should select such a term to describe her relationship with God. In this choice of words we catch a glimpse of the motivation that guided her through the rough waters that lay ahead.

Mary loved God, and because she loved God she wished to serve Him, no matter what the cost. In essence what she was saying was, "Lord, in light of all that you've done for me, this, as personally demanding as it is, is the least I can do in return."

God at the Movies

This simple exercise in relational logic was one of the first lessons I had to learn the night I gave my life to Christ. For a number of months I had been attending a Fellowship of Christian Athletes group that met at my high school on Friday mornings before class. Not that I was particularly interested in spiritual things, mind you, but my football coach (who was also my physics teacher) helped run the group. Since my playing time and my physics grade needed all the help they could get, I figured that showing up at an early meeting couldn't hurt. Occasionally the things talked about made an impression on me, but by and large I was convinced that I was doing just fine without getting too excited about this Jesus stuff.

One week the group decided to go to a Billy Graham film. A number of my friends were going, so I decided to show up as well. We definitely weren't in an overwhelmingly spiritual frame of mind when we arrived at the shopping center where the movie would be shown. As a matter of fact, several of us found our way into a record and magazine store of questionable reputation prior to the time we were to meet at the theater. Straightening our halos, we left that seedy place and met the rest of the group outside. Fully loaded down with popcorn, soft drinks, and enough candy to keep a dozen dentists in business for years, we tromped down the aisleway, found some good seats, and prepared for some mild entertainment.

The film was called *A Time To Run*. The basic message was that God is "the hound of heaven." Once He gets on our trail, He won't let up, no matter what we say or do, no matter how hard we fight. He will be satisfied with nothing less then total surrender to His love and presence in our lives.

Much to my surprise, I found myself strongly relating to the main character in the story. In fact, his constant efforts to keep God at arm's length seemed like the story of my life. Some of the conversations, relationships, and events seemed so familiar it made me wonder (in a flash of paranoia) if some of Billy's staff had been following me around for awhile. I mean this movie was too close to my life and attitudes about God for comfort.

The movie suggested an idea that had never crossed my mind before. The message was clear and unmistakable; not only was God real, but He loved me personally. During a concert scene, a song was performed that hit me like a ton of bricks. Its simple words expressed the idea that when Jesus died on the cross, he was saying, "I love you."

At that moment something inside clicked. My football coach had given a talk a few weeks before on the crucifixion of Christ from a doctor's point of view. He shared the conclusion that Jesus was so badly beaten before He even got to the cross that one could hardly recognize Him as a human being. This notion had rattled some of my preconceived, Renaissance art–inspired ideas of what the suffering of Christ was really like. But to think that in the midst of all that suffering and pain He loved me, some nobody high school kid from Oxnard, was almost too much to comprehend. For the first time in my life, sitting in a movie theater, I felt the love of God speaking to my heart saying, "Yes. I went through all that for you."

The movie came to an end, and, as is the custom at Billy Graham–sponsored events, they offered this invitation: "If you would like to commit your life to Christ, get up out of your seat and come to the front. A counselor will be available to talk with you about your decision."

My first thought was "No way I'm going to do that. My friends will think that I've flipped out. My coach will think that I'm a big hypocrite for going to these meetings all this time and not being a Christian..." I could think of at least eighty great reasons why walking down that aisle was the last thing on earth I should do. But, amazingly, deep in my heart I sensed God saying, "Get up and go on down there."

Suddenly it hit me.

I had prayed before (usually for divine intervention on a test grade or survival at football practice), but in reality my prayers were more good luck charms and expletives than any meaningful communication with the Almighty. The first words I ever said to God in prayer and really meant in my heart were, "In light of all You've done for me, this is the least I can do."

The True Meaning of Christmas—Part One

In Mary's heart–felt response to God, we can grasp an important piece of the puzzle that is Christmas. At Christmas we commemorate the entrance of the Son of God into the world. But Christmas should be more than simply a veneration of an event in history; Christmas should challenge us to examine our lives.

When we begin to consider the human impact of the birth of Christ, the hard decisions and tough commitments that this event generated, we are led to take a good long look at where we stand on crucial spiritual issues. Is our response to God one of gratitude and a desire to do His will in our lives and in our relationships? Or is God somehow an after thought to us, an aspect of life that we will certainly get around to seriously considering some— day, but not right now? Christmas is a vivid reminder that the living God who made all things has demonstrated His love and concern for us by becoming one of us, by taking on humanity in the person of Christ.

With this in mind, Mary's response is one of incredible, inescapable relevance to you and me. In light of all that God has done, how have we responded? Not in some emotionally charged moment of gratitude and well— intentioned commitment, but in the true crucible of our day–to–day lives? Francois Fenelon summed up where the rubber meets the road in our relationship to God: "It is not a question of how much we know, how clever we are, nor even how good; it all depends on the heart's love. External actions are the results of love, the fruit it bears; but the source, the root is in the deep of the heart."

Christmas asks us a pointed question. Have we experienced the love of God personally? Our response to God in the other 364 days of the year provides the answer. Mary's response revealed the attitude of her heart, "Behold, the bondslave of the Lord; be it done to me according to your word."

Christmas and Joseph

As you've probably guessed, Mary wasn't the only ordinary individual to be caught up in these extraordinary circumstances. She was engaged to a young man who would soon find himself drawn into a whirlpool of emotional confusion and conflict. His name was Joseph, "Now the birth of Jesus Christ was as follows. When His mother Mary had been betrothed to Joseph, before they came together she was found to be with child by the Holy Spirit. And Joseph her husband, being a righteous man, and not wanting to disgrace her, desired to put her away secretly" (Matt. 1:18–19).

For some strange reason we assume that people living back in the time of Christ were somehow more blindly accepting of the outrageous than those who live in the rarefied intellectual atmosphere of our day. My culturally biased set of assumptions told me that when Mary broke the news to Joseph about this incredible turn of events, Joseph simply looked piously upward and declared, "The Lord moveth in mysterious wayeths, doth not he?"

Nothing could have been further from the truth. As well–known writer C. S. Lewis insightfully comments:

> *You will hear people say, "The early Christians believed that Christ was the son of a virgin, but we know that this is a scientific impossibility." Such people seem to have an idea that belief in miracles arose at a period when men were so ignorant of the course of nature that they did not perceive a miracle to be contrary to it. A moment's thought shows this to be foolish, with the story of the virgin birth as a particularly striking example. When Joseph discovered that his fiancee was going to have a baby, he not unnaturally decided to repudiate her. Why? Because he knew just as well as any modern gynecologist that in the ordinary course of nature women do not have babies unless they have lain with men. No doubt the modern gynecologist knows several things about birth and begetting which Joseph did not know. But those things do not concern the main point—that a virgin birth is contrary to the course of nature. And Joseph obviously knew that.*[32]

Joseph had a firm grip on the facts of life. And when Mary told him the news of God's message, his reaction was human through and through. "O.K. Fine. You're telling me that God decided to make you pregnant. I don't want to make a big deal out of this, but I simply don't buy your story, Mary. I just can't handle this. I want out."

One can only imagine how Mary felt at that moment. Have you ever been in a situation where something happened that you considered really significant? Our immediate reaction is to share such important news with those we love. We assume that they will have the same understanding and sense of excitement about the event that we have. There are few experiences more devastating than to discover that those closest to us are either indifferent, skeptical, or even cold to our highlight experience.

Joseph's very understandable reaction undoubtedly hit Mary like a strong left hook. Instead of shared joy, there was an awful sense of aloneness and separation. As Joseph walked away his hopes and dreams for a future with Mary had crumbled in a pile of ashes. The love he felt for her was consumed by feelings of jealousy, anger, and betrayal. His only recourse was to end the relationship, as discreetly as possible.

> *But when he had considered this, behold, an angel of the Lord appeared to him in a dream, saying, "Joseph, son of David, do not be afraid to take Mary as your wife; for that which has been conceived in her is of the Holy Spirit. And she will bear a Son; and you shall call His name Jesus, for it is He who will save His people from their sins." Now all this took place that what was spoken by the Lord through the prophet might be fulfilled, saying, "Behold the virgin shall be with child, and shall bear a Son, and they shall call His name Immanuel," which translated means, "God with us." And Joseph arose from his sleep, and did as the angel of the Lord commanded him, and took her as his wife, and kept her a virgin until she gave birth to a Son; and he called His name Jesus* (Matt. 1:20–25).

The nine months between Mary's announcement and the birth of Jesus were certainly no emotional or relational cakewalk for Mary and Joseph. Even after being assured by an angel that this whole thing wasn't the world's lamest excuse for an unwanted pregnancy, even after shoring up

their commitment and love for each other, Joseph and
Mary had to live in an all–too–real world.

Think of all the knowing winks, the cruel and cutting
innuendos, the self–righteous glares of disapproval they
endured when they followed through with their wedding.
Think of all the doubts and sleepless nights that slowly
passed waiting for this child to be born.

Undoubtedly, during the "down" times, Joseph must
have glanced toward heaven and wondered, "Why us? Of
all the people in the world. Couldn't this have been done
some other way?" But, remarkably, Joseph hung in there.
He kept the faith, even when life and the will of God
didn't make a whole lot of sense to him.

The True Meaning of Christmas—Part Two

Many people are talking about faith these days. Just the
other morning I caught one of those down–home Brille
Creme preachers telling his enraptured audience that "faith
is the key to getting what you want out of life."

I'm rapidly becoming convinced that almost the exact
opposite is true. The more I look at how God works in the
lives of people, the more I believe that faith is not the key
to a luxury limo ride through life. Rather, this elusive
quality called "true biblical faith" is the fine art of trusting
in God's love and wisdom even in outrageously difficult
circumstances.

If we are honest with ourselves, this is no easy task.
More than once in this crazy world we will find ourselves
in Joseph's shoes. We will glance toward heaven and
mutter, "God, I just don't understand. *What* are You
doing? Why is all this happening?"

For us, the answers might not be forthcoming. Few
people I have met can claim to have heard the doorbell ring
and found an angelic messenger on the front porch. "Good
morning. Angel–Gram. Moment–by–moment diagram of
your life from the Almighty. Complete with graphs and

flow charts. Sign here, please." The sad reality is that when hard times come our way they are often accompanied by an almost palpable sense of spiritual silence. We find ourselves feeling quite alone facing a host of self–doubts and accusing thoughts, while even our most fervent and sincere prayers seem to bounce straight back to us off the ceiling. Even if we were to make a connection with heaven, we feel that we would probably end up talking to an answering machine.

Yet, as difficult and confusing as our time on earth can get, there is hope for those who put their trust in Christ to sustain them. The anxious sense of not knowing, not understanding God's plan for our lives, is a temporary burden to bear. Paul expressed it this way: "For now we see in a mirror dimly, but then face to face; now I know in part, but then I shall know fully just as I also have been fully known" (1 Cor. 13:12).

The implications of this promise are staggering. To put this in its proper perspective, consider for a moment what it will be like the first day we hit heaven. It's an interesting exercise to think about what our first words will be on that day when "faith will be sight." We've all heard the jokes about asking God the answers to unanswerable questions ("So tell me God, why are there twelve hot dogs in a package, but only ten hot dog buns?"). But when we begin to think through the prospect of actually standing before the Almighty, more serious sentiments come to the surface.

Some feel they will be stunned and speechless when confronted with the awesome majesty of the Lord in all His power and beauty. Some of the more expressive among us will probably shout, "Hallelujah!" Some of the more pessimistic might say, "I can't believe we're really here. We really made it after all." But I'm convinced that most of us will have an experience that is quite different. After years of struggling with the ups and downs of human existence, of desperately trying to make sense of it all, we will gaze upon the Lord, bathed in the full radiance of His wonder and wisdom and love, and with mouths agape we will utter these less than profound, less than poetic words: "Oh… I get it now."

So the second important lesson that Christmas can teach us is about trust. Even when things are most chaotic, we are never alone. Joseph, through the school of hard knocks, learned to hold on to a simple, yet fundamental truth. "And we know that God causes all things to work together for good to those who love God, to those who are called according to His purpose" (Romans 8:28).

Christmas and Jesus

It is clear that the first Noel, that gathering that looks so peaceful and serene in the plastic nativity scenes, knocked lives for a loop. Mary and Joseph endured an incredible load of social, relational, and spiritual pressure as God's plan unfolded.

But lest we forget, another individual was affected by this remarkable chain of events. No less a personality than God the Son, Jesus Christ Himself. "And it came about that while they were there, the days were completed for her to give birth. And she gave birth to her first–born son; and she wrapped Him in cloths, and laid Him in a manger, because there was no room for them in the inn" (Luke 2:6–7).

This setting is familiar turf for most of us. So familiar, in fact, that we often miss the full impact of what is so matter–of–factly reported here. The most outstanding personality ever to grace our planet with His presence, the fullness of God dwelling in human flesh, was born in a musty, stinky, insect–ridden, Middle–Eastern cow stall. His first cradle was no less than a carved–out limestone feeding trough. Hardly accommodations fit for a King.

The Royal Dumpster

To put the staggering implications of all this into proper perspective, it is helpful to compare the nativity of Christ with the birth experiences of more modern royalty. Imagine for a minute that Prince Charles has scheduled a visit to your hometown. Along for the trip is his wife, the lovely Diana, Princess of Wales. Di is expecting a child who could become the king of England. Although she is far along in her pregnancy, the doctors have assured her that she has more than enough time to complete the tour with Charles and return to Britain to give birth to the royal heir. Unexpectedly, the princess goes into labor early. How would the local dignitaries react? We would undoubtedly expect them to take the princess to the most excellent, state–of–the–art medical facility available. The number one obstetrician in the country would be flown in to supervise the birth. Every possible contingency would be anticipated and dealt with because, after all, this is no average child coming into the world. This is a royal birth.

Now imagine a starkly different turn of events. Charles and Di are driven past our state–of–the–art hospital complex. Instead of arriving at a high tech medical facility, they are driven to the worst part of town, led to the back of a fleabag hotel and left to make themselves at home by the dumpster. "Good luck! Hope this baby thing all works out. Don't worry. It's no big deal. Babies are born every day!"

How do you suppose Charles and Diana would feel at that point? No anesthesia. No doctors. No clean facilities. Just the two of them left all alone in a filthy parking lot. Perhaps Charles would be able to find an old used mattress in the trash to make things more comfortable.

If you can imagine that, you can get a small inkling of what the birth of the King of Kings, Jesus Christ, was like. And if this process was no picnic for Joseph and Mary, imagine what it must have been like for Jesus.

This all–too–vivid scenario raises a compelling question: Why do such a thing? What could have possibly motivated Christ to leave heaven in all its glory and splendor for such incredibly wretched poverty? A famous passage from the New Testament book of Philippians provides an eye–opening insight.

> *Have this attitude in yourselves which was also in Christ Jesus, who, although He existed in the form of God, did not regard equality with God a thing to be grasped, but emptied Himself, taking the form of a bond-servant, and being made in the likeness of men. And being found in appearance as a man, He humbled Himself by becoming obedient to the point of death, even death on a cross. Therefore also God highly exalted Him, and bestowed on Him the name which is above every name, that at the name of Jesus every knee should bow, of those who are in heaven, and on earth, and under the earth, and that every tongue should confess that Jesus Christ is Lord, to the glory of God the Father* (Phil. 2:5–11).

Give Me a Reason Why

Why go through such an ignominious birth? For that matter, why face firsthand the rottenness of life on this fallen world? Why face rejection and misunderstanding, even the excruciating pain of crucifixion? The reason was love. Jesus loved us so much that no sacrifice, no inconvenience, no humiliation was considered too great if it meant reaching lost, confused, frustrated, and spiritually lonely people like you and me. As Dorothy Sayers observed, "He has Himself gone through the whole of human experience, from the trivial irritations of family life and the cramping restrictions of hard work and lack of money to the worst horrors of pain and humiliation, defeat, despair and death. When He was a man, He played the man. He was born in poverty and died in disgrace and thought it well worthwhile."[33]

The True Meaning of Christmas—Part Three

In the last few years I have had the opportunity to talk with people who have been literally run over by life. One crushing blow followed another, dreams failed, shining potential became dull and then tarnished. Others have watched as relationships that promised to last forever crumbled and sifted through their hands like sand. Still others have stood by helplessly as friends or loved ones fell victim to pain, disease, and death. When these people hear about a God who loves them, we could almost excuse their indignancy. "God loves me? If He loves me so much, why doesn't He do something for me? Not something somewhere over the rainbow, but something practical. Something that really makes a difference. Something real."

This is the true meaning of Christmas. The Christ child, wrapped so tightly in swaddling clothes in a crude limestone cradle, is God's ultimate practical expression of love to those of us who suffer. God is not a God aloof and far away, but One who has entered into the full spectrum of life, the same life that you and I have to live. He sympathizes with our struggles and weaknesses, having, in the best and fullest sense of the phrase, walked a mile in our shoes. The message of Christmas is one that does not lend itself well to plastic and waxwork figurines. It is the message that God loves us, so much so that he became one of us, walked among us, and has felt the height of our joys and the depth of our pain. The message of Christmas is that God is the One we can talk to and never have to say, "You know what I mean?" He always knows what we mean. And He cares.

The Moral of the Story

It's been nearly two thousand years since that first Christmas morning. A lot of family gatherings have come and gone, and a lot of stockings have been hung by the chimney with care. A lot of Christmas dinners have been served, with a lot of leftover turkey sandwiches put away in the days that followed. A lot of children have greedily torn to shreds the paper that mom wanted them to save. A lot of carols have been sung, and a lot of junior high pageant participants have fretted their hour upon the stage.

But underneath all the noise and commercialism, a simple message has gone forth during the holidays. So simple, so sublime, it often goes unheard. But for those who take time to pause and reflect, to consider the meaning beneath the cliches, the message still remains. In his book, *A Layman Looks at the Son of God*, W. Philip Keller aptly sums up the bedrock meaning beneath the Christmas holiday season.

So she had her little baby all alone. Only Joseph was near. The sheep corral, filthy as only an Eastern animal enclosure can be, reeked pungently with manure and urine accumulated across the seasons. Joseph cleared a corner just large enough for Mary to lie down. Birth pains had started. She writhed in agony on the ground. Joseph, in his inexperience and unknowing manly manner, did his best to reassure her. His own other tunic would be her bed, his rough saddlebag her pillow. Hay, straw, or other animal fodder was nonexistent. This was not hay or grain–growing country. Stock barely survived by grazing on the sparse vegetation that sprang from the semidesert terrain around the town. Mary moaned and groaned in the darkness of the sheep shelter. Joseph swept away the dust and dirt from a small space in one of the hand–hewn mangers carved from the soft limestone rock. It was covered with cobwebs and debris fallen from the rock ceiling. There, as best he could, he arranged a place where Mary could lay the newborn babe all bundled up in the swaddling clothes she had brought along. There, alone, unaided, without strangers or friends to witness her ordeal in the darkness, Mary delivered her son. A more lowly or humble birth it is impossible to imagine. It was the unpretentious entrance, the stage entrance of the Son of man—the Son of God, God very God in human guise and form upon earth's stage. In the dim darkness of the stable a new sound was heard. The infant cry of the newborn babe came clearly. For the first time deity was articulated directly in sounds expressed through a human body. Those sounds brought cheer and comfort and courage to Mary and Joseph. These peasant parents were the first of multiplied millions upon millions who in the centuries to follow would be cheered and comforted by the sounds that came from that voice.

God is come. God is with His people. Immanuel.[34]

This is the true meaning of Christmas. God, up close and personal.

Joy to the world.

The Lord has come.

For me and for you.

Discussion   Questions

1. Read Luke 2:1–20. If you could have been any of the onlookers in the Christmas story, who would you choose to be and why?

2. Of Mary, Joseph or Jesus who had the toughest role to play in God's plan? Explain your answer.

3. Why do you suppose we surround the Christmas story with so much tradition and commercialism?

4. Read Hebrews 4:14–16. Does it effect you personally to know that God experienced life just the way we do? In what ways?

CHAPTER XI
HEAVEN ON $125 A DAY

Old man, exhausted by ordeal, detached from human deeds, feeling the approach of the eternal cold, but always watching in the shadows for the gleam of hope.

— Charles De Gaulle —

"IT ISN'T a question of if, but when." Those sobering words fade to a distant whisper when a young man stands face–to–face with a shining metal seductress called by a most unfeminine, yet irresistibility alluring name— "Motorcycle."

Breathes there a man with soul so dead that hasn't at least once imagined himself effortlessly weaving his way through gridlocked, evening rush hour traffic, wind in his hair, an adoring model–type holding onto his waist for dear life?

For these and far more pedestrian reasons, I fell victim to the siren's song and finally made up my mind that I would give way to my baser instincts and buy a motorcycle. The largest obstacle standing between me and the open road was selling the idea to my wife. Predictably, when I gingerly worked my way up to sharing my intentions, she looked at me like I had decided to sign up for the Evel Knievel School of Body Part Rearrangement.

"You're so accident prone you end up in the emergency room after flag football games. And you want to buy a motorcycle?"

I knew in a flash, the open–road–wind–in–your–hair– Easy–Rider angle wouldn't score big points in this particular conversation, so I opted for the responsible budget–conscious approach.

"Oh, come on. Accidents happen when people aren't paying enough attention. I know how dangerous these things are. I'll be on the alert all the time. Besides, motorcycles get great gas mileage, we'll save on insurance and repairs..."

She was looking more and more unconvinced by the second. I knew my only chance was to pull out all the stops and use the dreaded "s" word.

"You see, honey, if I ride a motorcycle, we'll have more money at the end of the month for projects, for trips, for... SHOPPING."

Although all common sense argued against it, I finally wore her down. Within two days I was the proud owner of a red Honda 550 with a nifty police–style, high–impact plastic windshield. For a minute I felt like I was five years old again, ready to hit the street for the first time—without training wheels. Born to be wild, man.

Then it hit me. Perhaps it was a premonition. Perhaps it was common sense talking. Perhaps it was a four–alarm case of buyer's remorse, but as soon as I sat on the custom leather seat of my new toy, the words of a friend who had been a motorcycle enthusiast for years came to mind. "Remember, Scott. Statistically *all* motorcycle drivers get into accidents sooner or later. Not just some, but all. It isn't a question of if, but when." I paused to mull that thought over, took a deep breath, and jumped on the kick starter. As I roared off around the corner and out on the open road, the warning faded. Accidents were for other riders; I would be extra–cautious. It wouldn't happen to me.

My caution served me well for the next six months. No problems. No accidents. Motorcycle riding had become a part of my L.A. freeway lifestyle. Zipping down the highway with the wind in my face (and the occasional bug in my teeth) was routine and almost second nature, until that late afternoon in early spring.

I was traveling on the fast lane of the Ventura Freeway in that awkward time when traffic is still moving along nicely, but rush hour is about to throw a magic switch and grind ten–mile trips into forty–five–minute ordeals. It had been a long day, and my mind was drifting ahead to getting home and taking a relaxing end–of–the–day jog on the fire roads that wound up into the hills behind our apartment.

Suddenly, the car in front of me slammed on its brakes. With a burst of adrenalin I tried to respond, but my bulky gloves would not allow me to reach the hand brake in time. At fifty–plus miles per hour my motorcycle smashed into the rear bumper of the now stationary Chevy in front of me and lurched to the left, careening toward the hard concrete of a lane addition under construction.

At that awful moment, a remarkable thing happened. It was almost as if the impact of the collision had literally ripped the fabric of time itself. For an instant, I felt like I had the leading role in an episode of "The Twilight Zone." Everything—the cars, my twisting motorcycle, even I—was moving in super–slow motion.

In the millisecond between the time I struck the car and hit the hard pavement, I found I had time to think, to evaluate, to assess the situation. I found myself saying, "Let's see. I've just struck a car. I'm going well over fifty miles per hour. There is no possible way to regain control, and I have a date with that newly hardened concrete to my left. My life is flashing before my eyes. Yep. This is it. I must be going Home. I am going to die."

The serenity of that instant was shattered when I struck the road. Holding on to the handlebars for dear life, I bounced a good three–to–five feet in the air, spun into the pavement, and, after about thirty–five feet, skidded to a stop. I have no idea how long I was out, but as I regained consciousness, I found myself pinned under the tangled mess that was my Honda 550.

Shock is a wonderful thing in moments like this. At first I couldn't feel a thing. Groggy as a boxer trying to convince his body to get up before the referee counts to ten, I tried to get a grasp on my situation. As I looked around I didn't see anyone in a white robe with a harp, so I figured I was still among the living. With a calmness that surprised me, I thought to myself, "Okay. I'm alive. I'd better take a quick inventory and see what kind of shape I'm in."

Like a quality control expert at an appliance factory, I checked the function of my limbs, one major appendage at a time. "Let's see here… right hand… all fingers working… right foot… toes still able to wiggle… left foot…"

At that moment the shock wore off. The searing pain that jolted me confirmed that my central nervous system was still hitting on all cylinders. Although the intensity of pain was well beyond anything I had ever experienced before, in an odd way I was relieved. High on my list of awful, potential consequences from an accident was the possibility of being paralyzed. Thank God I could still move and feel. On the downside, the kick stand of the motorcycle had pierced my left shoe and was imbedded deep in my ankle. Certainly not the most pleasant way to spend an afternoon.

As I lay helplessly pinned under some three–hundred pounds of wrenched metal, waiting for some passerby to stop or at least summon the highway patrol (no help arrived for some ten minutes), it dawned on me that my motorcycle veteran friend was right. My moment had come. When it came to an accident, no matter how much I rationalized or kidded myself, the old adage held true. It wasn't a matter of if, but when.

Some Impressive Statistics

The "not if, but when" principle doesn't apply only to fledgling, accident–prone motorcyclists. Sooner or later each of us will face a similar crisis when our confident veneer of invincibility and immortality is stripped away, and the afterlife stretches out before us, breathless and overwhelming. Sooner or later, each of us must face what the Bible refers to as "the last enemy"—death.

Unfortunately, death is a very present reality—a fact of life we have real problems handling. Our culture does its best to either hide death behind the calm, antiseptic walls of the hospital or old folks home, or we simply try to deny its true seriousness by poking fun at it through the media. We numb ourselves to its inescapable presence by burying it under a latex and paint–filled garbage heap of movie and television special effects, the gorier and more outrageous the better.

Neither of these popular approaches bothers death in the least. It goes about its business twenty–four hours a day, seven days a week. Consider for a moment that in the United States alone, it is estimated that over two million people will die this year. That's over 167,500 per month... 5,580 per day... 232 per hour... and since you began to read this chapter nearly twenty people have passed into eternity. Playwright Oscar Wilde once observed, "The statistics on death are most impressive. One out of one people die." In other words (to paraphrase my motorcycle–riding friend's rule of thumb), statistically, if you are breathing today, you will eventually face death. It is not a question of if, but when.

A Myth is as Good as a Mile

In the preceding pages of this book, we have operated on the assumption that myth is alive and well, and thriving in our culture.

We have attempted to compare conventional wisdom concerning spiritual matters with the truth of God's Word. And, as we near the end of this examination, a very pointed, yet reasonable objection might be rolling around. "Great. What the average man on the street believes about spiritual issues is radically different than the message of the Bible. But, honestly, what real difference does it make? How does something as vague and intangible as belief make a practical difference in day–to–day life?"

Let me speak candidly. As has been mentioned in previous chapters, Jesus Christ changes lives in a markedly practical way. Becoming a Christian is the beginning of a wonderful process in which God begins to mold, shape, and refine our character. He will not be satisfied with us until our thoughts, actions, motivations, and even our ability to love are a living reflection of Jesus Himself.

Yet we have all met people of other faiths, or no faith at all, who seem to be getting by rather nicely in life. And as long as circumstances proceed in a smooth, predictable way, there may seem to be little difference in quality of life between the Christian and the nominal or non–Christian.

Death, however, completely scrambles that equation. Death takes our beliefs and assumptions and puts them to the test. When the "death dew lies cold upon our brow," religious subjects like the existence of God and an after–life are yanked away from the theoretical and speculative, and made as unavoidably relevant as a 1040 EZ form. Dorothy Sayers, in her book *Christian Letters to a Post Christian World*, sums up the issue:

> In ordinary times we get along surprisingly well, on the whole, without ever discovering what our faith really is. If, now and again, this remote and academic problem is so

unmannerly as to thrust its way into our minds, there are plenty of things we can do to drive the intruder away... But to us in wartime, cut off from mental distractions by restrictions and blackouts, and cowering in a cellar with a gas mask under threat of imminent death, comes in the stronger fear and sits down beside us.

"What," he demands rather disagreeably, "do you make of all this?... What do you believe? Is your faith a comfort to you under the present circumstances?"

We may not face restrictions and blackouts and cowering in a cellar, but sooner or later we will face death. What will we believe about that? How will we cope when the "not if, but when" comes around to visit us personally? Into which basket will we eventually place all our proverbial eggs?

The Approach of Fantasy

Some people say that opinion is the queen of virtues. If this is true, then these days personal experience must be the king. Countless contemporary discussions of truth come to a screeching halt when one person plays the ultimate rhetorical trump card: "Yes, I can see how a person who hasn't gone through it could feel that way, but this happened to me. I've experienced it personally." Argument over. Case closed.

Our love affair with personal experience is having a marked impact in many different areas of life, most notably our view of death. Some are attempting to brace for the inevitability of death by putting their faith in a number of all-too-personal subjective experiences.

Near Death Experiences

Research tells us that approximately one-third of the people who nearly die, or who briefly experience "clinical death"—a loss of vital signs—and are revived, have what is known as a Near Death Experience (NDE). According to a 1982 Gallup survey, nearly one out of every twenty adult Americans has had an NDE.

While specific details vary, the following account reported by a woman named Carlene Huesgen is representative:

> One afternoon, I quietly slipped out of my body and went up to the corner of the room. It seemed all right and I had no desire to go back. I saw people around the (hospital) bed, working on my body, but I was not that interested in it. "Why are they wasting their time?" I wondered. At the opposite end of the room was a long, dark tunnel and to the left of it was the most beautiful white-gold light. There aren't adequate words to describe it. It was very loving, it was all-knowing and it was what I communicated with. All I had to do was think of a question and I had the answer. It transferred knowledge to me about things I wanted to know.
>
> I had no fear. I wanted to go with it and be with it, and it let me know that if I went through the tunnel I would be permanently leaving my physical body—and that was OK. I was raring to go.[35]

The great popularity of belief in NDE–like scenarios about death is easy to understand. Who wouldn't want to view death as a warm and loving experience with no pain, no strain, no fear involved? A beautiful light at the end of a tunnel is there to greet us, and as one NDE reporter put it, "all our problems are over." Yet, before we place our hope of life–after–death squarely on the shoulders of this phenomena, there are some rather shaky aspects of NDEs that need to be addressed.

First, near death experiences are usually intensely personal in nature. No one has ever shared in or objectively verified an NDE. Add to this the fact that the NDE almost always takes place during a time of great physical difficulty and is strongly linked to altered states of consciousness. The reliability level of the observer is at best questionable under such circumstances. Was this experience a real brush with the supernatural or simply a hallucination brought on by a lack of oxygen, reaction to medication, stress, or a whole list of other factors?

Secondly, NDE's are just that—*Near* Death Experiences. They occur during a thirty–second to five–minute crisis period where heroic attempts at reviving the body are taking place. As such, one may be told that they were "clinically dead" for a brief period of time due to absence of measurable vital signs, but under such circumstances pronouncing a person dead is, at best, an inexact science.

Being specific about the precise moment of a person's death remains a gray area. This point was recently driven home in the hallowed halls of the American judicial system. According to the Associated Press, a jailhouse lawyer named Jerry Rosenberg attempted to use this vagueness and uncertainty as a legal loophole. Some twenty–five years ago, Rosenberg was tried and convicted of first degree murder and subsequently sentenced to life in prison. In 1986, during coronary bypass surgery his heart stopped on the operating table. After a few minutes his heart was restarted by the attending physicians. Rosenberg's case was simple and somewhat ironic. He contended that during that crisis his life ended, and thus he had served his life sentence. In his appeal he tried to convince the judge that our modern definition of death was ambiguous and that there were "two kinds of death, reversible and irreversible." In essence what Rosenberg was saying was, "Look, the courts told me to stay in prison until I died. Well, I did that. Why can't I go free? After all, I held up my end of the bargain!"

Cayuga County Judge Peter Corning called Rosenberg's NDE defense interesting, but not convincing. "As his presence in this courtroom indicates... he did not die."[36]

What common sense points to, the case of Jerry Rosenberg makes explicit. A Near Death Experience is definitely in the eye of the beholder. It is completely personal; completely subjective. No expert can say for certain, "Yes. You definitely passed into the 'Great Beyond' and came back to tell the tale." Common sense also tells us that there is a vast difference between such instances of recovery after two or three minutes and a person sitting up at his or her funeral three days later and describing life beyond the grave. However alluring such NDE accounts may be, death is too serious and final a prospect to face with our hope built on such an uncertain foundation.

Looking Forward by Looking Back?

Another approach to ultimate reality that is grounded in the purely subjective has captured both prime time programming and top spots on the New York Times Best Seller List. With high profile spokespersons like Shirley MacLaine at the forefront, the New Age Movement has gone from an esoteric religion of the love generation to achieving the ultimate measure of cultural prominence— being the butt of jokes on "The Tonight Show."

The essence of the New Age message on death? Don't worry about death—you've been through it before.

This point was driven home with appropriately mystic overtones on an edition of "2 On the Town," a television magazine show produced by the CBS affiliate in Los Angeles.

On February 28, 1985 program host Melody Rogers promised viewers "...a very enlightening edition of '2 On the Town.'" The subject of the program? Reincarnation. As the show progressed, viewers were introduced to Dr. Thelma Moss, faculty member of the psychology department at UCLA. Dr. Moss specializes in a technique known as "Regressive Therapy" in which a patient is placed under hypnosis and guided back to "past lives" and "experiences before birth." Moss remarked that those who have been involved in transcendental meditation and guided imagery are particularly good subjects for this exercise. Since Melody Rogers was an avid participant in both of these "religious" pursuits, the greater Los Angeles viewing public would get an opportunity to watch a regressive therapy session firsthand.

Those looking for a brush with the metaphysical were certainly not disappointed. Rogers described being a doctor in the British army, as well as her experiences as an Indian living in a tepee. The highlight of the session came as Rogers was brought to the point of one of her former "deaths." She described the process of passing away as "seeing just white . . ." and being "good... real fast."

Although Moss charges $125 per session (and $650 a week to learn to become a "regressive therapist"), there was no shortage of customers willing to pay for her time. A high price tag for a subjective experience? Undoubtedly.

Other psychologists such as Dr. William Unger took a rather dim view of all this supernatural excitement. "One can dream about anything read about or encountered in daily experience. This is not scientifically valid."

Still this common sense observation did not dampen the fervor of the true believer. One patient stated, "It wouldn't matter if it really was a past life, it was wonderful." Another added, "It was true enough in my own mind so it satisfied me."

This same fervor for information from the great beyond has created what may go down in history as the most ridiculous fad since streaking flashed across the public consciousness. I refer to that high–tech, modernized, and yuppified version of the seance, trance channeling. Popularized by Shirley MacLaine in her book and ABC mini–series *Out On A Limb,* people claiming direct psychic hook–up with personalities ranging from UFO jockeys to deceased relatives have sprung up across the country.

Like the six–year–old who convinces himself that all burglars are really nice people so he can sleep at night, many attempt to still their fear of death by buying into professionally–guided, hypnotically–induced, and often outrageously expensive fantasies. Those who cannot afford sessions with Dr. Moss can build their faith in past lives through such popularly–priced spiritual aids as the supermarket tabloids. (Sample headline: "Reincarnation Proven—Baby Born with Pirate's Peg Leg.") Again, the unrelenting reality of death is too serious a matter to trust to the realm of guided dreams, make–believe, or the studied counsel of "a minor radio personality who is sitting with his eyes closed and his fingers locked in little circles talking in an accent that is faintly reminiscent of Donald Duck." Yet many today are attempting to face death simply by making just such a leap to the mystical and subjective.

The Approach of Fatalism

On the other side of the coin, there are those in our popular culture who opt for a hard–bitten, bite–the–bullet, and face–the–facts approach to death. The essence of this "life's a pain and then you die" school was captured by novelist Raymond Chandler. "What did it matter where you lay when you were dead? In a dirty sump or in a marble tower on top of a high hill? You were dead, you were sleeping the big sleep, you were not bothered by things like that. Oil and water were the same as wind and air to you. You just slept the big sleep, not caring about the nastiness of how you died or where you fell."[37]

The message? Life is too short to waste time worrying about death. When it happens it's all over anyway so forget about it. It will happen soon enough.

The problem with this tough–it–out–and–live–for–today school of mortality is found in its effect on day–to–day living. Almost inescapably, our view of life is profoundly influenced by our view of death. This came through loud and clear in *Life* magazine's end of the year issue for 1988. In a special holiday feature called (humbly enough) "The

Meaning of Life," the approach of fatalism—that death is the inevitable end of everything—was well represented. Consider the words of taxi driver Jose Martinez:

> *We're here to die, just live and die. I drive a cab. I do some fishing, take my girl out, pay taxes, do a little reading, then get ready to drop dead. You've got to be strong about it. Life is a big fake. Nobody gives a ——. You're rich or you're poor. You're here, you're gone. You're like the wind. After you're gone, other people will come. We're gonna destroy ourselves, nothing we can do about it. The only cure for the world's illness is nuclear war— wipe everything out and start over.*[38]

From the world of entertainment comedian Jackie Mason adds:

> *Life has no meaning beyond this reality. But people keep searching for excuses. First there was reincarnation. Then refabrication. Now there's theories of life after amoebas, after death, between death, around death. Now you come back as a shirt, as a pair of pants.... People call it truth, religion; I call it insanity, the denial of death as the basic truth of life. "What is the meaning of life?" is a stupid question. Life just exists. You say to yourself, "I can't accept that I mean nothing so I have to find the meaning of life so that I shouldn't mean as little as I know I do."*[39]

And finally, in a glimmer of hope against hope, writer Charles Bukowski declares, "I am my own God. We are here to unlearn the teachings of the church, state and our educational system. We are here to drink beer. We are here to kill war. We are here to laugh at the odds and live our lives so well that Death will tremble to take us."[40]

The meaning of life? Buck up. Keep a stiff upper lip. "Be happy, don't hurt other people, and hope you get the chance to love somebody."[41] The "big sleep" is coming for all of us and that ends everything. No more you; no more me. Since life is one colossal accident, non–existence might just be a relief. So party hearty, and don't worry about how many people get stepped on in the process.

The seemingly brave new, fatalistic approach to death—in essence, life means nothing, so enjoy the trip— works well, as long as death maintains a comfortable distance. But when the end begins to draw near, this bold perspective often changes. As the brilliant French philosopher and avowed atheist Voltaire lay upon his death bed, he turned and addressed his attending physician: "'I am abandoned by God and man. I will give you half of what I am worth if you will give me six months' life.' The doctor replied, 'Sir, you cannot live six weeks.' Voltaire turned to the doctor and declared, 'Then I shall go to hell, and you will go with me.' Soon after he expired."

One need not be at death's door to experience the same sense of awful foreboding. Tennessee Williams once remarked, "Whether or not we admit it to ourselves, we are all haunted by a truly awful sense of impermanence. I have always had a particularly keen sense of this at New York cocktail parties, and perhaps that is why I drink martinis almost as fast as I can snatch them from the tray. Fear and evasion are the two little beasts that chase each other's tails in the revolving wire cage of our nervous world."

Clearly, bravado and bluster are lost on death. Our proud assertions of independence or indifference do little to slow down its inevitable arrival in our lives.

A Third Option

We have seen that imagination and even the most heroic emotional declarations of independence are hopelessly ineffective when confronting the raw reality of the here–after. Some weigh both of these alternatives and see that they are sadly lacking. Like a freezing man desperately trying to start a fire with a book of water–logged matches, many believe that man is hopelessly ill–equipped to deal with the prospect of his own demise. Fortunately, there is another alternative that allows us to rationally and confidently face the grave.

As we have seen in previous chapters, God Himself has revealed truth to man through the Bible. The Old and New Testaments are far more than a reliable, inspiring piece of devotional religious literature. Their message is eminently and inescapably practical, particularly when it comes to the subject of death. It has been accurately observed that fear and the unknown often go hand–in–hand. By taking a look at the message of the Bible we can dispel such fears by gaining a reliable grasp on what death and dying are all about and what destiny awaits us on the other side.

An Inevitable Destination

Because the Bible is a book concerned with spiritual issues, it should not surprise us that death and the afterlife are prominent within its pages. Although there are many excellent passages that can give us insight into death, much of the biblical perspective on this issue is summed up in a very brief, yet profound verse found in the New Testament book of Hebrews. "And inasmuch as it is appointed for men to die once and after this comes judgment" (Heb. 9:27).

A One–Shot Deal

Perhaps the most eye–opening aspect of this statement leaps out at us from the very outset. The Bible insists that death is a one–time event in the life of every person. No room is allowed in this equation for the concept of reincarnation. As romantic as it is to think that we previously lived as heroic warriors, dedicated physicians, or Indian princesses (isn't it interesting that past lives are always seen as glamorous—no one ever seems to claim they were a scullery knave or a cockroach the last time around), such is not the case. We do not keep returning until we "get it right." In a heady dose of spiritual realism, the Bible insists that this life, and this life alone, will decide our destiny in the hereafter.

Our Day in Court

The second key point we can glean from this passage is also cause for thought. After death we will not face a glowing golden tunnel or the Elysian Fields. We will find ourselves face to face with God Himself. C. S. Lewis captures vividly the drama of that moment awaiting all of us:

> *For this time it will be God without disguise: something so overwhelming that it will strike either irresistible love or irresistible horror into every creature. It will be too late then to choose your side. There is no use saying you choose to lie down when it has become impossible to stand up. That will not be the time for choosing: it will be the time when we discover which side we have really chosen, whether we realized it before or not. Now, today, this moment, is our chance to choose the right side. God is holding back to give us that chance. It will not last forever. We must take it or leave it.*[42]

Between Heaven and Hell

Lewis's vivid portrayal of our ultimate moment of truth provides deep insight into an issue that has troubled and confused many for centuries. The Bible explicitly tells us that each and every individual will stand before God and give an account of his or her life. If this is true, the most important question we can ask is: What will the standard of judgment be?

Some have already made up their minds on this issue. One student I spoke with remarked, "Hey, I'm a pretty good guy. If God grades on the curve I'll make it." This is a popular perspective in our culture. The Gallup organization has discovered that over two–thirds of all Americans think their chances of getting to heaven are good. Many envision God as being like a doddering, half–senile grandfather figure in the sky, smiling and muttering under his breath as the entire sea of humanity past, present, and future flows by his heavenly easy chair and into the pearly gates.

The Bible presents a significantly different picture of Judgment Day.

> And I saw a great white throne and Him who sat upon it, from whose presence earth and heaven fled away, and no place was found for them. And I saw the dead, the great and the small, standing before the throne, and books were opened; and another book was opened, which is the book of life; and the dead were judged from the things which were written in the books, according to their deeds... And if anyone's name was not found written in the book of life, he was thrown into the lake of fire (Rev. 20:11-12, 15).

At this point some crucial questions are raised. "Wait a minute. You've been telling me chapter after chapter that the only way to get to heaven is by putting my trust in Jesus and relying on God's grace—not my own good deeds. But here God is judging people 'according to their deeds.' What's the story?"

An Order in the Court

As we have already discussed, God has given man the precious gift of free choice. This total freedom extends even to the way we choose to approach God. In this crucial choice there are two avenues open to us: We can either admit that we are incapable of pleasing God through our own good deeds and put our trust in Christ's death and resurrection on our behalf, or we can attempt to earn our place in heaven by our own works. John's vision of an event called the Great White Throne Judgment confirms a startling fact. God will honor our free choice even on Judgment Day. God will in fact judge us based on our own way of relating to Him. If we put our trust in Christ, we will be judged in Christ's merit. If we put our trust in good works or rituals or being above average on a moral curve, we will stand before God with only these things to recommend us. Our righteousness will be compared to God's exacting standard of perfection. This standard is a high one to attain. As James 2:10–11 says, "For whoever keeps the whole law and yet stumbles in one point, he has become guilty of all. For He who said, 'Do not commit adultery,' also said, 'Do not commit murder.' Now if you do not commit adultery, but do commit murder, you have become a transgressor of the law."

This clear statement is literally on a collision course with our popular conception of sin and living an upright moral life. A recent *People Magazine* survey came up with what was called "The Sindex: a reader's guide to misbehavior."

Are hypocrites worse than tattlers? Are tax cheats more sinful than industrial spies? To answer these and other metaphysical mysteries, *People* asked readers how guilty they would feel, on a scale of one to ten, if they engaged in any of fifty–one activities. The results were averaged to give each behavior a Sin Coefficient (Adultery, for example, earned a 7.63) and a ranking in the Reader's Morality Index.

Murder	9.84
Rape	9.77
Incest	9.68
Child Abuse	9.59
Spying against your country	8.98
Drug Dealing	8.83
Embezzlement	8.49
Pederasty	8.30
Spouse Swapping	8.09
Adultery	7.63[43]

Clearly, we differentiate between sins. Some are terrible. Some not so bad. Some we write off to human nature. And while there is a case to be made for specific sins to be worse than others based on consequences for our lives and the lives of those around us, all sins large or small, overt or hidden deep in the heart, have one damning effect. In this respect the little white lie is in a real sense no different than first degree murder. Both violate God's law. Both separate us from a Holy God. We choose to go our own way and our choice matters—forever. If we refuse to accept God's offer of forgiveness, we will be judged by our own deeds and found sadly wanting. As Christian author Cliffe Knechtle put it:

> *The only reason people are going to hell is because all life long they have told God that they can live just fine without Him. On the judgment day God will say, "Based on your own decision to live life separately from Me, you will spend eternity separate from Me." That's hell. God will not violate our will. If all life long we have said, "My will be done," then on the day of judgment God will say to you, "your will be done for eternity." G. K. Chesterton put it this way: "Hell is God's great compliment to the reality of human freedom and the dignity of human choice."*[44]

Oh, Yeah? Says Who?

According to the Bible, death will finalize the decision we have made concerning our relationship with God. For those who know God, who have received His forgiveness and restoration by trusting in Christ, heaven in all its wonder awaits.

At times Christians have been chastised (and perhaps rightly so) for being all too ready to talk about hell and strangely vague and silent when it comes to heaven. What will heaven be like? The Bible provides mind-boggling glimpses of heaven's utter beauty, tranquility, and joy. We often find ourselves hungering, ironically enough, for a more physical description of an essentially spiritual place. Our longings are met with an incredibly enticing promise: "Things which eye has not seen and ear has not heard, and which have not entered the heart of man, all that God has prepared for those who love Him" (I Cor. 2:9).

Yet heaven's greatest attractiveness is not found in geography, architecture, or aesthetics, but in personality. Jesus Christ said, "And this is eternal life, that they may know Thee, the only true God, and Jesus Christ whom Thou hast sent" (John 17:3). In essence, if you love God, you'll love heaven, because He is heaven's main attraction. There we will see Him face to face.

For those who reject a relationship with God through Jesus Christ, eternal separation—an existence completely devoid of God's provision, blessings, and grace—awaits; a place the Bible calls hell.

Unlike the ego–massaging allure of "regressive therapy" or the bedtime–story warmth of an NDE, the biblical view of death and the afterlife hits us with the cold wind of truth, of decisions to be made and consequences to be weighed, of real life.

To be sure, the notion of once–to–die–and–then–comes– judgment is a difficult thing to accept. It is entirely fair to ask on what authority such claims are made.

The precedent for the biblical view of death does not rest on emergency room hallucination, hypnotic auto– suggestion, or head–in–the–sand bravado. The Christian view of death, as well as all of Christianity, stands or falls on a historical event—the resurrection of Jesus Christ from the dead.

One of Scripture's most extensive and specific discussions of the afterlife is found in the book of 1 Corinthians, chapter 15. Introducing the entire subject of death and the hereafter, the apostle Paul wrote:

> *For I delivered to you as of first importance what I also received, that Christ died for our sins according to the Scriptures, and that He was buried, and that He was raised on the third day according to the Scriptures, and that He appeared to Cephas (Peter), then to the twelve. After that He appeared to more than five hundred brethren at one time, most of*

whom remain until now, but some have fallen asleep; then He appeared to James, then to all the apostles; and last of all, as it were to one untimely born, He appeared to me also. (I Cor. 15:3–8)

God has not been subtle in providing substantial verification that He has revealed Himself through Jesus Christ. Who better to consult on the afterlife than:

- One who died in a moment of history. The death of Jesus Christ had to be certified by four official Roman executioners before His body could be taken down from the cross. John's eyewitness account tells us that a guard rammed a spear through Christ's rib cage, and blood and water flowed out. Writing in the *Journal of the American Medical Association*, Dr. William Edwards observed:

  The important feature may not be how he died but rather whether he died. Clearly the weight of historical and medical evidence indicates that Jesus was dead before the wound to his side was inflicted and supports the traditional view that the spear, thrust between his right ribs, probably perforated not only the right lung but also the pericardium and heart and thereby ensured his death. Accordingly interpretations based on the assumption that Jesus did not die on the cross appear to be at odds with modern medical knowledge.[45]

- One who literally rose from the dead in a moment of history. Professor Thomas Arnold, holder of the Chair of Modern History at Oxford once observed, "I have been used for many years to study the histories of other times and to examine and weigh the evidence of those who have written about them, and I know of no one fact in the history of mankind which is proved by better and fuller evidence of every sort, to the understanding of a fair inquirer, than the great sign which God hath given us that Christ died and rose again from the dead."[46] (To more fully explore the evidence for the literal, physical resurrection of Christ, I encourage you to read *Jesus Christ: The Witness of History* by Sir Norman Anderson and *The Resurrection Factor* by Josh McDowell.)

- One who three days after death appeared to real people—not just an inner circle of secret admirers but over five hundred individuals at one time who subsequently bore witness to the event. As *Time* magazine noted, "Conservatives also make a historical case for the bodily resurrection of Jesus. Dean John Rogers of Pennsylvania's Trinity Episcopal School for Ministry points out that St. Paul's account of Jesus' appearances after his resurrection (1 Corinthians 15) was written only two decades after the events and drew on prior accounts. Says Rogers: 'This is the sort of data that historians of antiquity drool over.'"[47]

Since none of us have gone through the process of death we find ourselves in the uncomfortable position of taking someone else's word for it. The question we must grapple with is simple, yet utterly challenging—Whose word will we take on the subject?

Will we opt for the absurdity and ultimate hopelessness of the "I–Did–It–My–Way" school of pop philosophy? Will we invest our hope in the latest spiritual fad of the Hollywood cocktail party scene? Will we put our trust in culture or tradition as we try to make sense of the clatter and din of a hundred different religious leaders, each claiming an exclusive lock on the truth? Or will we stop and realize that only Jesus, who has truly died and truly risen from the dead, has the experience and the authority to give us trustworthy information? When we consider the inescapability and ultimate consequences of death, it only makes sense to place our faith in the one who experienced it fully and brought it down to defeat, once and for all?

Eternity Observed

The call came a little before nine on a comfortably cool November evening. My grandfather, Ralph Osborne, had been hospitalized following a stroke about ten days before this still, southern California night. His condition had stabilized over the last few days, bringing an Indian summer of hope that the strong and vigorous patriarch of our family would rally, and life would return to normal.

It was not to be.

I had just finished speaking to a high school youth group when I was handed a note that simply said, "There's been a turn for the worse. Come to the hospital." With a calm that betrayed numbness, I gathered my things and jogged to my car. About twenty minutes later I arrived, to be greeted by my dad who shared the bad news. "Grandad is back in Intensive Care. It doesn't look good."

After a short time we were told we could go in for a minute to see my grandfather. The network of clear tubing and electrical equipment surrounding him seemed brutally ironic. Here was a man who spent his whole life supporting and caring for others, now on total support. Unconscious, yet still alive.

We left the room and began to wait. As members of the family sat in the hospital lounge, little was said. A few sincere words of support and encouragement would occasionally break the silence, but the atmosphere, heavy with a sense of impending loss, seemed to leave such expressions dry and awkward, more socially appropriate than emotionally helpful.

A few minutes later the word came. The man who had taught me how to bowl and to drive, how to enjoy the subtle drama of listening to a Dodger game on a sultry, late August afternoon, and how to enjoy the not–so–subtle humor of a good practical joke—was gone. Grandad had passed away.

A strange sense of unreality hung in the air as we made our way slowly back to the room in the ICU. Grandad gone? For good? It made as much sense as someone claiming that from here on out sunrise had been canceled. With every step toward Intensive Care a large part of our lives, a good part of our lives, seemed to be washing away, and there wasn't a thing we could do to stop it.

As we filed in, it struck me that something was strangely, yet unmistakenly different in the room, even from a few minutes before. The life support equipment had been disconnected and removed, and at first I thought that was what I was sensing. But a restlessness in my mind would not allow me to be satisfied with that conclusion.

No, it was something more. Something personal. My gaze focused on Grandad's body, lying on the hospital bed. As I looked at him, I realized something that I will carry with me to my death. Grandad was gone.

Everything that had made this man Grandad was clearly absent. As I looked at his face, a face I knew well from many years of bristly–five–o'clock–shadow–hugs, it was as if another person was lying there. More than just animation, all that strange, immeasurable, unquantifiable "something" that leaves philosophers scratching their heads, what the common man calls a soul, had left. Seeing this man whom I loved so deeply, less than ten minutes after death, solidified in my mind the validity of an oft repeated cliche. The real you and the real me is more than just this incredible tangle of neurons and blood vessels, muscles and skin, knee caps and hangnails. Who we truly are lies deep within. And who we really are does not die with the body. I walked away from Pleasant Valley Hospital on that cool, cloudless night absolutely convinced of two irrefutable facts. There was no doubt that I would grieve for the loss of Ralph Osborne. Death had inflicted a terrible, terrible blow to our family.

But the life story of a man we admired, laughed with, and loved deeply wasn't over.

Grandad had faced death. Now he stood before the just and loving God. Once to die, after that the judgment.

The Heart of the Matter

In the final analysis, faith is not a side issue. What we believe about God and how we relate to Him matters more than anything else. I close this book with a warning and a piece of very practical advice. What we half believe can hurt us. Buying into a set of spiritual convictions based on "They say . . ." and, "I heard once . . ." or, "That's how God looks to me" is a recipe for disaster. Personal frustration in the here and now, and permanent separation from God in the hereafter are in store unless:

- We have the intellectual integrity and honesty to take a hard look at spiritual issues. To ask: What do I really believe about God? Why do I believe it? Can I take an honest look at the life and teachings of Jesus Christ and dismiss Him as simply a nice teacher, a prophet, or the product of an over–active Galilean imagination? Is there more to Jesus than that?
- We have the personal integrity and honesty to take a hard look at our own lives. Where do I stand with God today? If my time came and he asked me, "Why should I let you into My heaven?" what would I say? Have I truly come to grips with my personal need and received God's forgiveness?

The practical piece of advice? It's not enough to know *about* God. It's only enough when we know Him personally. As we have already discovered, this is a relationship we must receive as a gift because it is far beyond our ability to earn. In the quietness of our hearts, we must ask ourselves three crucial questions.

Have I come to grips with the fact that I am not living a life that pleases God, that I am separated from him by true moral guilt? The Bible tells us that "all have sinned and fall short of the glory of God" (Rom. 3:23). If we are still busy trying to rationalize and justify ourselves, Christ cannot help us. As He said, "It is not those who are healthy who need a physician, but those who are sick.... I did not come to call the righteous, but sinners" (Matt. 9:12, 13b).

Have I come to grips with the fact that Jesus Christ loved me enough to die on a cross to pay the price for my wrongs? This is the true basis of a real relationship with God. In 1 John 4:9–10 we read, "By this the love of God was manifested in us, that God sent His only begotten Son into the world so that we might live through Him. In this is love, not that we loved God, but that He loved us and sent His Son to be the propitiation for our sins."

Finally, has there ever been a time in my life where I consciously, as an act of my will, asked God to forgive my sins, to come into my life, and to make me the person He wants me to be? The Bible says, "But as many as received Him (Jesus), to them He gave the right to become children of God, even to those who believe in His name" (John 1:12).

If you would like to know God in a personal way, you may do so by expressing this desire to Him through prayer. God is not so much concerned about the words we use as the attitude of our heart. Simply take a moment to admit your need of forgiveness:

- To acknowledge what Jesus has done for you in making forgiveness possible, dying on the cross in your place;
- To receive Christ's forgiveness personally, as a free gift;
- To ask God to come into your life and begin the incredible process of making you like Christ.

The last dangerous myth the world taught me can be summed up in four simple words: "I'll Get Right Later."

The Bible says, "'At the acceptable time I listened to you, and on the day of salvation I helped you; behold, now is the acceptable time, behold, now is the day of salvation'" (2 Cor. 6:2).

We need no longer rely on myths and second guessings to understand the meaning of life, and to know and love God. He hears our claim to be honest seekers of truth and calls our bluff by sending His Son to teach truth, to embody truth, to confirm truth with the awesome attestation of the empty tomb. To a world neck–deep in the tar pits of opinion and relativistic confusion, He holds out a simple, unmistakenly invitation: "And you will seek Me and find Me, when you search for Me with all your heart" (Jer. 29:13).

Clearing away all myth, excuse, and distraction, God asks each of us an ultimate question:

"Where do you stand with Me today?"

Discussion Questions

1. Read II Corinthians 5:1–10. Have you ever come face to face with death? How did the experience effect you?

2. Is the average person in our society ready to die? If God told you had one hour to live how would you feel? What would you do with the time?

3. A friend shares that they are planning to make their peace with God on their death bed. How would you respond?

4. If you were to die tonight and God were to ask, "Why should I let you into my Heaven?" What would you say?

Footnotes

1   Reprinted from *The Vanishing Hitchhiker, American Urban Legends and Their Meanings*, by Jan Harold Brunvand, by permission of W.W. Norton and Co., Inc. Copyright 1981 by Jan Harold Brunvand. 62.

2   Ibid., 81.

3   Ibid., 22.

4   Ibid., 1-2.

5   George Gallup Jr., "Who Delivered the Sermon on the Mount?" Quoted in *Tabletalk*, Vol. 12, No. 1, February, 1988, 5. Copyright 1988, Gannett News Service. Adapted with permission.

6   Bob Green, *Chicago Tribune* (October 20, 1987).

7   Thomas A. Sancton, "Planet of the Year," *Time* (January 2, 1989), 30.

8   Charles R. Swindoll, *Growing Deep in the Christian Life* (Portland, OR: Multnomah Press, 1986), 202.

9   *Associated Press* (December 11, 1987).

10   J. Dwight Pentecost, *Things Which Become Sound Doctrine* (Westwood, NJ: Flemming H. Revell Co., 1965), 17-18.

11   Cliffe Knechtle, *Give Me an Answer* (Downers Grove, IL: Inter-Varsity Press, 1986), 39.

12   Ibid., 111.

13   Susan Shaeffer Macaulay, *How to Be Your Own Selfish Pig* (Elgin, IL: David C. Cook Publishing Co., 1982), 78. Used with permission by David C. Cook Publishing Co.

14   William Pfaff, "University Crisis," *Los Angeles Times* (January 2, 1989).

15   Bruce Newman, "Hype," *Sports Illustrated* (January 23, 1989), 62- 67.

16   Richard N. Ostling, "Who Was Jesus?" *Time* (August 15 1985), 37.

17   Ibid., 41.

18 Gleason L. Archer, *Encyclopedia of Bible Difficulties* (Grand Rapids, MI: Zondervan Publishing House, 1982), 342. Copyright 1982 by The Zondervan Corporation. Used by permission.

19 Josh McDowell and Don Stewart, *Answers to Tough Questions* (San Bernardino, CA: Here's Life Publishers, 1980), 80.

20 Ibid., 35.

21 For further information, I'd encourage you to read *When Skeptics Ask*, by Norman L. Geisler and Ronald M. Brooks (Wheaton, IL: Victor, 1990).

22 John Leo, "A Holy Furor," *Time* (August 15, 1988), 34.

23 Ibid., 35.

24 B. Westcutt and F. J. A. Hart, *Introduction and Appendix to the New Testament in the Original Greek*, vol. I (London: MacMillan, 1896).

25 F. F. Bruce, *The New Testament Documents: Are They Reliable?* (Downers Grove, IL: InterVarsity Press, 1984), 15.

26 Richard N. Ostling, "Who Was Jesus?" *Time* (August 15, 1988), 39.

27 William Whiston, translator, *The Works of Josephus Complete and Unabridged* (Peabody, MA: Hendrickson Publishers, 1988), 480.

28 Pierre Sauvage, "Jesus as a Boy," *Jerusalem Post* (September 24, 1988), 22.

29 Kate Desmet, "Jesus Interview Goes Beyond Scripture" *Gannett News Service* (April 28, 1988).

30 Sir Norman Anderson, *Jesus Christ: The Witness of History* (Downer's Grove, IL: Inter-Varsity Press, 1985), 70.

31 C. S. Lewis, *Mere Christianity* (New York: MacMillan Publishing Co., 1960), 55-56.

32 C. S. Lewis, *Miracles* (New York: MacMillan Publishing Co., 1960) 48.

33 Dorothy L. Sayers, *Creed or Chaos?* (New York: Harcourt Brace and Co., 1949), 4.

34 W. Phillip Keller, *Rabboni* (Old Tappan, NJ: Flemming H. Revell Co., 1977), 56-57.

35 Dodie Gust, "Near Death," *Arizona Daily Star* (April 27, 1985).

36 Associated Press (June 24, 1988).

37 Raymond Chandier, *The Big Sleep* (New York: Vintage, 1976), 215-216.

38 Brian Lanker, "The Meaning of Life," *Life* (December, 1988), 80.

39 Ibid., 83.

40 Ibid., 84.

41 National Broadcasting Company, *Family Ties*, "They Can't Take That Away From Me," pt. II, air date April 9, 1989.

42 C. S. Lewis, *Mere Christianity* (New York: MacMillan Publishing Co., 1960), 66.

43 Unattributed, "Sin," *People* (February 10, 1986), 107-109.

44 Cliffe Knechtle, *Give Me an Answer* (Downers Grove, IL: Inter-Varisty Press, 1986), 42.

45 William D. Edwards, MD; Wesley J. Gabel, MDiv; Floyd E. Hosmer, MS. AMI, "On the Physical Death of Jesus Christ," *Journal of the American Medical Association*, Vol. 255, No. 11, 21 March 1986, 1462. By permission of Mayo Foundation.

46 Thomas Arnold, *Sermons on the Christian Life—Its Hopes, Its Fears and Its Close*, 324.

47 Richard N. Ostling, "Who Was Jesus?" *Time* (August 15, 1988), 41.

OTHER RESOURCES

For more insights into how to effectively share God's love with a doubtful world, see Scott Richards' book, *Answers for the Skeptic*, available through The Word For Today.

Other books with related topics include...

The Claims of Christ, by Chuck Smith

The Gospel According to Grace, by Chuck Smith

The Creator Beyond Time & Space, by Mark Eastman & Chuck Missler

Practical Christian Living, by Wayne Taylor

If you would like to contact the author to learn more about the Christian faith, please write to him at:

Calvary Christian Fellowship of Tucson
3850 N. Commerce Drive, Suite 113
Tucson, Arizona 85705
(520) 292-9661

For a complete catalog of available books, videos, music products, and more, please contact The Word For Today at P.O. Box 8000, Costa Mesa, California 92628 or call toll-free 1-800-272-WORD(9673).